Oasis

Executive Editor: **Mike Evans**
Editorial: **Michelle Pickering, Karen O'Grady**
Production: **Michelle Thomas, Melanie Frantz, Mark Walker**
Picture Research: **Maria Gibbs**
Design Supervision: **Penny Stock, Leigh Jones, Geoff Borin**
Design: **Design Revolution, Brighton**

Special thanks to:
Johnny, Christine and Karen at Creation Records

Record sleeve design & art direction by Brian Cannon for Microdot,
photography by Michael Spencer Jones

This edition published in 1997 by Hamlyn, an imprint of
Reed Consumer Books Limited, Michelin House, 81 Fulham Road,
London SW3 6RB and Auckland, Melbourne, Singapore and Toronto

Picture Acknowledgements

All Action / **Gareth Davies** 62 top / **Justin Thomas** 68–69
/ **USP** 80 below, 80 top

Alpha 79 / **Mark Allan** 78 main

Apple Corps Ltd. 50

George Bowstead 15

Brian Cannon / **Microdot** 9, 17, 25, 35, 44, 45, 55

Creation Records / **Andy Wilsher** 10 bottom

Fiona Hanson / **PA News** 62 bottom

Melody Maker / **Piers Allardyce** 8 below / **Grant Peden** 8 top
/ **Pat Pope** 5, 38 all, 42 / **Tom Sheehan** 11, 29, 30–31, 31 bottom, 32,
33, 34 / **Stephen Sweet** 7 / **Ian Tilton** 13 top,

Redferns / **Kieran Docherty** 73 / **Mick Hutson** 39, 40, 72 top
/ **Steinwehe** 26 / **Des Willie** 64 main, 65

Retna / **Steve Double** 20, 22 top left, 22 top right, 67 / **Chris Floyd**
63, 70 / **Niels van Iperen** 74 main / **Sam Mack** 66 / **Tony Mottram** 16
/ **Scarlet Page** 74 inset / **Joe Ramsay** 78 inset top right / **Robin** 6
/ **Paul Slattery** 71

Rex Features 75 / **Brendan Beirne** 77 / **Brian Rasic** 72, 76
/ **Ph. J. Sutton-Hibbert** 59 top right

S.I.N. / **Piers Allardyce** 21 top / **Martin Goodacre** 21 bottom
/ **Hayley Madden** 56 / **Tony Medley** 4, 47 / **Roy Tee** 49 bottom

Paul Slattery 3,10 top, 12 all, 13 centre, 13 bottom, 14, 18, 19 right,
19 left, 22 bottom, 23 all, 24, 27 all, 28 all, 30 left, 36–37, 41, 43,
46 all, 48, 49 top, 51, 52, 53 all, 54, 57 all, 58, 59 bottom, 59 top left,
60 bottom, 60 top, 61

Oasis

PAUL LESTER

HAMLYN

CONTENTS

★★★★★★☆☆ ★★★★★★★★

The Rain
'Your music's shite'

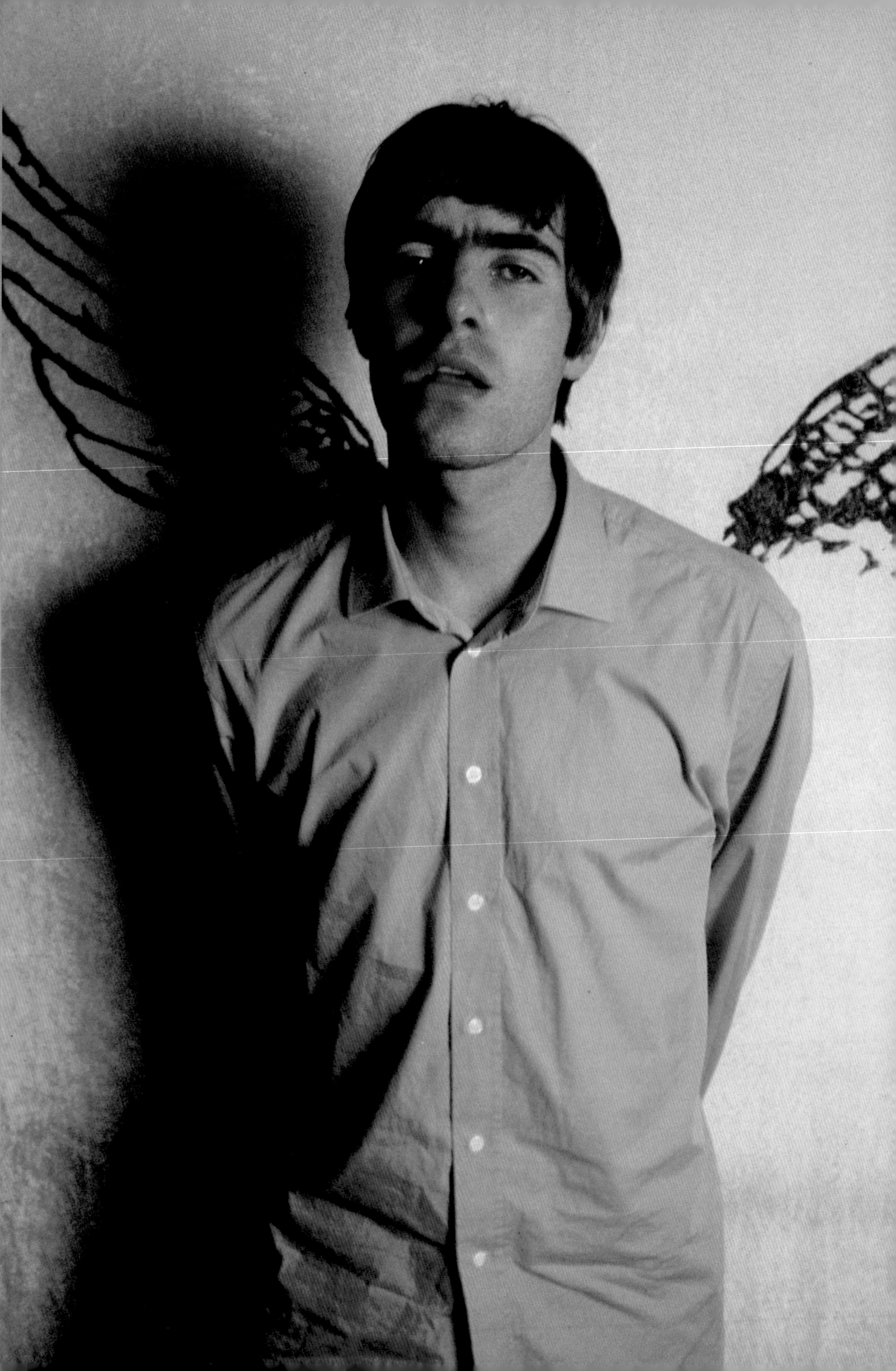

Manchester: so much to thank it for . . . the Gallagher brothers' teenage years . . . the baggy scene takes over in the city . . . Noel and Liam see The Stone Roses and find God . . . Noel roadies for the third Madchester band, Inspiral Carpets . . .

AS is so often the case, as it was with The Beatles and The Rolling Stones, as it is with all the bands who have gone on to break records and enter the history books, the early part of the Oasis story is slow and punctuated with false starts.

The story stretches back to the turn of the decade. In many ways, you could attribute the staggering success of Oasis to fellow Manchester band, The Stone Roses.

It was at one particularly memorable hometown Roses show in early 1990 that the germ of the idea of forming a band probably first crossed the minds of the hugely impressed Liam and Noel Gallagher, the ('extremely lapsed Catholic') sons of Irish parents who were brought up in Burnage, a pleasant but fairly dull suburb of South Manchester.

Not that Liam Gallagher, at this point 22 (he was born on September 22, 1972), had ever been a big fan of music. He was more into getting off with girls, playing football and scoring draw, which he first did at the tender age of 14.

'I didn't give a fuck about music,' says Liam. 'Anyone that walked past me with a guitar would get loads off me: "You fuckin' freak. You weirdo, playing music." I just thought it was all weird.'

The older Gallagher brother Noel, who was born on May 29, 1967, was definitely into music; he had been ever since the early Eighties, when he discovered punk. He would bunk off lessons at school, burgle a bit, dabble in adhesives, drink cider and listen to The Sex Pistols.

The Stone Roses at their peak, Alexander Palace, November '89

'I was completely out of fuckin' control,' recalls Noel. 'I didn't give a shit.'

When he was 13, Noel and a friend robbed their local corner shop. He was put on probation and his parents grounded him for six months. This gave Noel the opportunity to practice on the acoustic guitar that his father, a Country & Western DJ, had given him when he was 12.

Before long, Noel had taught himself to play Beatles songs, despite a handicap he shared with his hero John Lennon, dyslexia.

While still a teenager, Noel saw The Smiths and was blown away by Johnny Marr's guitar-playing. The only other guitarist to have a similar impact was John Squire of The Stone Roses. It was at a Roses gig that Noel approached a bloke who was in the crowd, taping the concert. It was Clint Boon of Manchester band The Inspiral Carpets. Boon invited Gallagher to be the Inspirals' roadie and guitar technician. Over the next two years, after quitting his job at British Gas, Noel travelled the world, to America, Japan, even Russia.

It was while he was in America, in 1991, that he phoned home, only to be told by his mum that Liam was in a band of his own, consisting of guitarist Paul 'Bonehead' Arthurs, bassist Paul 'Guigs' McGuigan and drummer Tony McCarroll. The latter three had been playing in an outfit called The Rain

Lad demi-gods, Happy Mondays

(not the Liverpool act of the same name). When Liam joined, they decided to change their name, taking it – depending on which story you believe – either from a Manchester bar, a clothes shop or a poster on a street wall. The name was Oasis. Back in Britain in January 1992, Noel checked out Oasis' debut performance at The Boardwalk. He was unimpressed, but he made his mind up: he was to be Oasis' leader, whether they liked it or not.

'I told our kid the band were shite,' said Noel, 'but that he definitely had something

Noel's first bosses in the music biz, Inspiral Carpets

as a frontman. Then I said, "You either let me write the songs and we go for superstardom, or else you stay here in Manchester all your lives like sad cunts." '

Talk about making them an offer they couldn't refuse! The band let Noel take control of the operation, leaving all songwriting (and, later, production) duties to their new mastermind. At last, Noel had an outlet for the songs he had been writing in his spare time with the Inspirals.

Not that Noel was ready to give up his increasingly frustrating day job – yet.

'The worst thing was knowing that I was better than the Inspirals were – miles better,' he says. 'But I needed the money and that's why I stuck it out, 'cos getting a band off the ground is difficult. Not that that really mattered. I knew I was going to make it, whatever – I was born to do this.'

Invigorated by his new-found sense of conviction, Noel bought Oasis' equipment and the band started rehearsing in a room under the Boardwalk. He finally gave up his roadie work to concentrate on his new band.

Noel's decision to go all-out with Oasis enabled them to play the occasional local pub gig, which they did, to the absolute disinterest of all and sundry.

Champagne Supernova-dom was still some way off.

★★★★★★ ★★★★★★★

'Supersonic'
'Give me gin and tonic'

oasis

Oasis in Moseley, March 1994

18 Wheeler

TUT TUT

SOMETHING just had to happen, and soon. No band with this much total belief in their own sheer brilliance could fail to make at least some waves.

The opportunity to make a bigger splash arose completely by chance in May 1993, after over a year of rehearsing and refining the Oasis sound. Sister Lovers were an all-girl Manchester group named after early Seventies US cult band Big Star's celebrated third LP-cum-monument to misery. Oasis had befriended Sister Lovers and, when the latter scored a support slot at Glasgow's King Tut's Wah Wah Hut with the Big Star-influenced band, 18 Wheeler, they hitched a ride with them all the way up to Scotland.

Having travelled hundreds of miles, however, Oasis realised they wanted a little more payback for their effort than two hours' worth of audience-mingling with several hundred Glaswegians. No, what Oasis wanted was to do what they were convinced they were put on Earth to do: to play live. So badly did they want to perform, in fact, that, after being politely told to wise up and piss off by the club's promoter, they threatened material damage, physical violence and all manner of carnage and general chaotic unpleasantness. Oasis were grudgingly allowed to play a short four-song set. The story may well have ended there had fate not intervened for a second time in one night. Because who just happened to have turned up early that evening to catch the support act and was standing unexpectedly in the crowd when Oasis appeared to perform their impromptu four-song slot? None other than Creation Records boss, Alan McGee, there to see his new signings, 18 Wheeler.

Oasis support 18 Wheeler in Glasgow and Alan McGee offers them a deal . . . Noel meets Johnny Marr and Oasis sign to Marr's management company . . . Creation Records beat off all-comers in signing the band . . . their debut single – 'Supersonic' – is released . . . meanwhile, trouble erupts in Amsterdam . . .

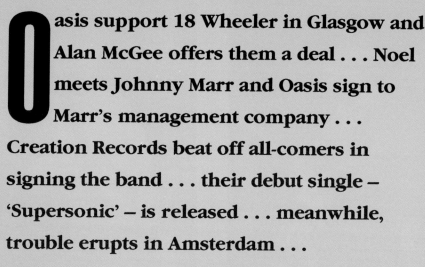

Legend has it that, before Oasis had even got to the end of their first number, McGee had poured half a bottle of Jack Daniel's over his head and was seen melodramatically clutching his heart, proclaiming Liam Gallagher to be the magical mix of John Lydon and John Lennon he'd been waiting for since the dawn of Creation, and

hailing Oasis as not only 'like The Jesus And Mary Chain if they'd been able to play their instruments' but also (albeit a hackned claim) 'the future of rock'n'roll'.

Then McGee allegedly surpassed himself for sheer unbridled, spontaneous lunacy when he jumped onstage and, cheque-book in hand, offered the band a five-album contract on the spot.

'He came up to us and went, "Have youse got a record deal, man?"' recalls Noel. 'And we went, "No." And he went, "D'youse want one?"'

Guigsy . . .

. . . Bonehead . . .

. . . and, um, Noely ?

MOVING ON UP

SO, after that bizarrely fortuitous four-song set – only their 20th gig thus far – Oasis were set to be part of what they considered to be 'the greatest rock'n'roll label in the world', the former resting place of leftfield renegades The Jesus And Mary Chain and innovative sound-weavers My Bloody Valentine as well as the current home of Primal Scream, Ride, Sugar and Teenage Fanclub (mind you, when the time came to sign on the dotted line in winter 1993, rumour has it that Noel would only put pen to paper if and when Creation did something about labelmates Slowdive, Swervedriver and Shonen Knife, who, reckoned Gallagher, were 'the biggest pile of shite I've ever heard in my life!').

Not that Alan McGee regretted his rash behaviour that night at King Tut's. And the indie majordomo was even more convinced when he received Oasis' demo cassette.

The cover of the tape was striking enough, featuring the band's now-familiar twisted Union Jack logo. And the music was nothing short of spellbinding. Included on the cassette (which is impossible to find nowadays, due to the fact that only about ten copies were made) are early versions of

'Fade Away', 'Married With Children', 'Columbia', 'Digsy's Dinner', 'I Will Believe', 'Alive', 'D'Yer Wanna Be A Spaceman?' and 'Bring It On Down'.

A few days after hearing the tape, Noel, Liam and Bonehead came down to meet the Creation posse in North London. But it was in their home base Manchester that Oasis got lucky for the third time in their short career. Noel had a chance encounter with a bloke he'd known from the Hacienda club simply as Ian, who happened to ask Gallagher for a copy of their demo so he could play it to his younger brother.

Ian's younger brother turned out to be Noel's hero from The Smiths, Johnny Marr! Marr heard the tape, came to see Oasis play at Manchester's Hop & Grapes, Marr told Marcus Russell (of Electronic's management company, Ignition) about this great new band he'd heard and Russell, after seeing them support Dodgy, offered to work for Oasis. (Equally exciting for Noel was that Marr gave him the guitar he used on The Smiths' best album, 'The Queen Is Dead', a Gibson Les Paul once owned by The Who's Pete Townshend!)

The cumulative effect of all this record company and management interest – not

forgetting the all-important first two reviews in the weekly music press, the *NME* review of their August gig at the Boardwalk celebrating the band's 'brilliant melodic framework', and the *Melody Maker* review (their first 'lead review', with a photo of Liam) of their September performance at the 'In The City' festival homing in on their 'exuberant, menacing freshness' and 'shimmery, rich sound' – was, simply, a bidding war of quite unrivalled ferocity. At one point, U2's Mother label allegedly promised to double any of the twenty or more other offers on the table.

Finally, on October 22nd 1993, Creation became the envy of every record label in Britain when Oasis signed to the label in the UK, with Sony picking up the rights for the rest of the world. There was just one problem to overcome before Noel put pen to paper, however – there were photos of Oasis' most hated band, quintessential baggy thug-rockers The Farm, on the wall at Creation HQ and they just had to go.

'I was like, I'm sorry, but we don't sign unless that picture's removed,' says Noel. 'They didn't take me seriously until I said: Look, I'm going to the toilet and I ain't coming out till it's gone. The Farm just rub us up the wrong way. They're chancers, but they think they're The Beatles.'

The band celebrated their signing, and the removal of the Farm snap, by entering what they now affectionately refer to as their 'Hamburg Period', hawking their wares around every toilet-venue in the land, supporting the likes of Verve, Liz Phair, The Milltown Brothers, St Etienne, The Real People and, as they put it, 'countless other shit bands'. The paying public generally remained indifferent to Creation's hot new signing, an indifference which helped the band hone to perfection a very useful 'no one likes us and we don't care' attitude.

Extremely useful, in fact, because, before the band had even reached stage one of their career – the debut single – the *NME* had tried to start the Oasis backlash, a live review of their Birmingham Institute gig in December describing Liam Gallagher as a 'vaguely Ian Brown-as-Tim Burgess slob of a frontman, singing in a vaguely tuneless half-whine, vaguely shaking a tambourine'. Liam later told another *NME* hack that if he ever met the reviewer in question, he would 'fuckin' slap the dick all around'.

That same week, however, *Melody Maker* rectified matters when journalist Calvin Bush gushed thus: 'They play eight songs, seven of which are more marvellous than Lena Olin in slinky black lingerie and a bowler hat. They are, frankly, incredible. They leave. I gasp and ache. The thought of having to wait a whole 10 days until they play here again is cramping my (life)style.'

I guess he liked them.

Naturally, there was far higher hyperbole to come . . .

'DAM BUSTERS

OASIS spent the first couple of months of 1994 in a variety of recording studios, attempting to get together enough tracks to be able to release a new single every two or three months a la The Beatles and the Stones, as well as enough for an album. The band zigzagged from Liverpool's Pink Museum, where they wrote what was to be their debut single 'Supersonic' in a mere

Liam gives it loads of frontman arrogance, September '93

Oasis hit the Midlands, March '94

Oasis' very own Buddy Rich, Tony McCarroll

eight hours, to Monmouth's £800-a-day Monnow Studios (where they just managed to run through a few ramshackle Rolling Stones covers with Noel on vocals), to the famous Olympic Studios in Barnes, to Cornwall's Sawmills Studios, to Manchester's Out Of The Blue, to Wales' Loco Studios, to London's Matrix.

And yet, in spite of all this gadding about, and apart from the 'Supersonic' sessions, hardly anything had been committed to vinyl – we were yet to hear Oasis on record. That said, in December 1993, those teasers at Creation did whet our appetites when they sent out to various press and radio types a white label promotional 12-inch of 'Columbia' from the band's demo tape. Radio 1FM took one listen to this raw mix of an already rough and ragged track and playlisted it, the first time they had ever done so with an unreleased song.

So we were at least getting some idea of what Oasis would sound like. In January 1994, 200 people had to be turned away from the band's debut appearance in the capital at the Water Rats in King's Cross, although the lucky few hundred who managed to do sardine impressions got to see what Liam, Noel, Guigs, Bonehead and Tony looked like.

And then, in February 1994, the third part of the puzzle started to fall into place when we got an opportunity to find out what Oasis were really like as people. There had already been reports of furious band in-fighting and fraternal imbroglios on the road with Whiteout earlier in the year, suggesting Oasis were the latest in a long line of hooligan rockers from the Stones to The Sex

A rare glimpse of Oasis smiling. Sort of.

Pistols to Frankie Goes To Hollywood to Happy Mondays.

But it was on February 18th, when the band were scheduled to support Verve in Amsterdam for their first ever gig outside Britain, that we got our first truly explicit view of The Real Oasis. Apparently, only Noel got off the ferry from Harwich. Liam and Guigs had reputedly got drunk on enormous quantities of champagne and Jack Daniel's and became involved in scuffles with security men and police, generally brawling and smashing up furniture along the way. Stated the *NME*: 'The pair were then handcuffed and locked in the brig.' The following morning, Bonehead awoke to find that his room had been ransacked and his passport and clothes stolen. He was also apprehended by the authorities for causing a disturbance along with Tony McCarroll after

loudly banging on the doors of numerous neighbouring cabins. Consequently, the four band members were placed in a dockyard cell upon the ferry's arrival in Holland, and then promptly deported by the local authorities. Poor old Noel was forced to make his way to the venue on his own and call off the gig.

Liam thought the whole incident was pretty funny and very rock'n'roll. Noel begged to differ.

'Nah, rock'n'roll is playing in Amsterdam, coming back, and telling everyone you blew 'em away,' he said. 'NOT getting thrown off the ferry like some scouse schlepper with handcuffs. That's just football hooliganism.'

'SONIC' BOOM
BEFORE their reputation for rucking could overshadow their reputation for, um,

Oasis storm *The Word*

rock'n'rolling, Oasis released their riotous first single 'Supersonic' in April 1994.

We had already been blown away by a live performance of the song on *The Word*, their TV debut, in March. Now we could bring the raw energy of this ravishingly exciting young band into our homes whenever we wanted with the band's new four-track Creation EP.

'Supersonic' itself was based around such a naggingly infectious chord sequence it was like you'd heard it before many times, and yet. already. it felt as much like Oasis as anything else. A simple celebration of hedonism and epic audacity ('Feeling supersonic/Give me gin and tonic' drawled Liam. easily the cockiest singer since Ian Brown), the words also offered a glimpse into Noel Gallagher's psychedelic imagination ('I know a girl called Elsa/She's into Alka Seltzer/She sniffs it through a cane on a supersonic train . . . she done it with a doctor on a helicopter'), pure John Lennon-circa-'I Am The Walrus'-meets-Shaun Ryder-esque lysergic whimsy.

Noel had a succinct explanation of the song's lyrics: 'It's just about some fucking nine-stone geezer who got Charlie'd off his nut one night.'

Of the extra tracks, 'Take Me Away' was a melancholy acoustic number sung by Noel with echoes of Harry Nillson's plaintive 'Everybody's Talkin'' (from the film *Midnight Cowboy*), 'I Will Believe' was a simple live rocker and 'Columbia' was the white label demo recording.

From the sleeve of the single – a wide angle shot of the band tuning up in the studio surrounded by guitars, amps and assorted equipment – to the music itself, it was clear from the off that Oasis were about Classic Rock'N'Roll, all cocky postures, delinquent braggadocio, insouciance that verged on arrogance, simply brutal (boorish?) rifferama and an almost Luddite aversion to the technological advances of the late 20th century.

The public didn't hesitate to demonstrate their own love of classic rock'n'roll when they sent 'Supersonic' soaring to Number 31 in the charts.

★★★★★ ★★ ★★★★★★★

'Shakermaker'
'It's the right time'

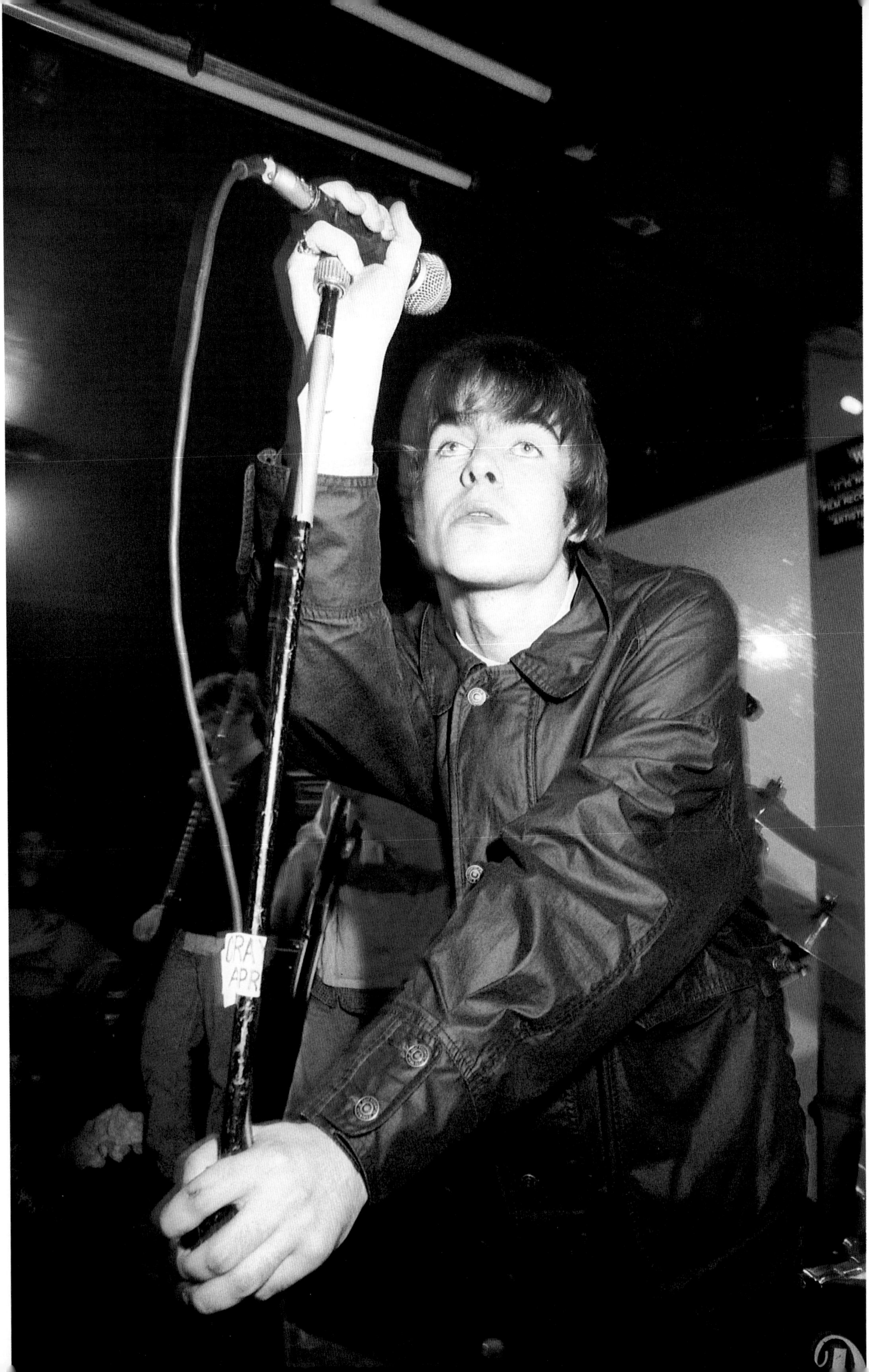

The brothers Gallagher seal their group's reputation as The Most Argumentative Band in Britain . . . second single 'Shakermaker' nearly gets the band sued by Coca-Cola . . . Oasis get to Number 11! . . . and appear on Top Of The Pops . . .

BROTHERS IN QUALMS

IT was in April that Oasis really cemented their dual reputations as The Best New Band In Britain – with 'Supersonic' as well as a series of ferocious live shows, notably their incendiary performance at the 100 Club in London's Oxford Street – and The Most Argumentative New Band In Britain.

It was their first major feature, in the *NME*, that brought to the nation's attention the extent of the damage these headstrong young brothers were prepared to do to each other. There was even a photo alongside the piece that showed Liam trying to take a swing at Noel.

Then there was the text . . .

First, there were the dazzlingly daft non-sequiturs:

Liam: 'You want to be Andrew Lloyd Webber, you do. You fucker.'

Noel: 'Who's Andrew Lloyd Webber?'

Liam: 'I haven't got a clue. He's a golfer, or something . . . I'm just an average lad who was born in Burnage, who played conkers.'

Noel: 'CONKERS?'

Liam: 'Conkers, mate. Conkers. The fucking lot. Conkers. That is it.'

Noel Gallagher, heir to Johnny Marr's throne ?

Oasis at legenaary haunt, the 100 Club

Then there was the heated exchange about the negative review of Oasis live the previous December by NME stringer, Johnny Cigarettes:

Liam: 'I'll slap him [Cigarettes] around the show.'

Noel: 'Shut up, man. SHUT UP!'

Liam: 'No, you shut up.'

Noel: 'No, YOU shut up.'

Liam: 'No, you shut up. If I ever meet the fucker, I'll slap him.'

Noel: 'You're talking shit.'

Liam: 'I'll hit him with a bottle, right in his kipper. I'll smash the fuck right out of him.'

Their future's so bright, they gotta wear . . .

Then things really got nasty:

'Let's fucking go, then, you DICK! Let's have a fucking FIGHT!' yelled Liam, offering to place a good, hard punch in his elder sibling's face as the journalist and press officer took an embarrassed back seat.

'I hate this bastard,' Liam ranted on, to no one in particular, pointing in the direction of Noel. 'And that's what it's all about. That's why we'll be the best band in the world, cos I fucking hate that twat there. And I hope one day there's a time when I can smash the fuck out of him. With a fucking Rickenbacker. Right on his nose. And then he can do the same to me.'

'How often do we argue?' Liam repeated the hack's question. 'Every day. Hourly. But it's not hate. It's love. I don't hate him. It's love. It's one of them. We're brothers, man. It's deep shit.'

Liam may have put down their frequent and furious bust-ups – which smacked (literally!) of the scraps 30 years previous between Ray and Dave Davies of The Kinks – to subconscious brotherly love, but, in an interview with *Loaded*, the Bible Of Lad, Noel had a different slant on matters fraternal.

'If I lived in America, I would have blown his [Liam's] head off by now and completely regretted it,' he was quoted in the macho mag. 'Since I live in England, though, I just give him a black eye or something every now and again. I don't hate him, but fuck me he pisses me off sometimes.

'Thing is,' Noel put forward his theory, 'Liam don't write no lyrics, he doesn't play any instrument, doesn't write nothing – so all he's required to do is stand there and sing and fucking look good. And I think he gets pissed off by the fact that he doesn't actually do anything because he can't. I dunno, I think he just winds me up on purpose, the cunt. I think it's just boredom. I don't know what to do. We can't even agree to disagree.'

Noel put it simplest in the style magazine *The Face*: 'He's a genius frontman and was born to do this. But he also wishes he was me. Always has done.'

Oasis were also shaping up as possibly the most ambitous, audacious and arrogant

Liam shakes his maker at New Cross, May '94

Oasis: so hard, they'll rob your hub-caps

The 'increasingly lunatic' Guigsy

new band in Britain – and that's just the 'A's – who rarely (if ever) let an occasion go by without making an outragous assertion about the band's brilliance and/or inevitable superstar status.

'We're the musical equivalent of Muhammad Ali,' they said in *The European*. 'I think we'll be the most important band in the world. We'll be the new Beatles,' the band informed the *NME*. 'We're the best band on the planet. That's not arrogance, that's just a fact,' they boasted in *Smash Hits*. 'Us and [Paul] Weller are the only real class on this bill,' they said of the Glastonbury 1994 line-up. 'I pity anyone who doesn't buy our records,' they told *Melody Maker*, adding that 'even The Stone Roses couldn't write a song like "Supersonic".'

And, as early as August, they were telling *Select* magazine that they would be Number One by Christmas '94 with the still-unrecorded 'Whatever'.

Thing is, most of their assertions weren't really all that outrageous when you thought about it – they were true.

Well, sort of, anyway.

COKE ADDICTS

OASIS, it was quickly becoming clear, were not afraid of anything, least of all controversy. Which was just as well, because they were attracting plenty of it.

Oasis know what time it is – literally!

They were teetering especially close to the edge with 'Shakermaker', their second single, released in June '94, due to its uncanny melodic resemblance to the ancient Coca-Cola jingle, the one sung by The New Seekers and used by the huge multi-national conglomerate as their early Seventies advertising campaign theme, 'I'd Like To Teach The World To Sing'. It was so similar, in fact, that Creation actually feared that the all-powerful Coca-Cola Corporation might consider suing them.

For quite a while, Oasis had actually appropriated the line, 'I'd like to buy the world a Coke', for live renditions of 'Shakermaker', and now the band's songwriter Noel Gallagher wanted to keep it on the recorded version. As far as he was concerned, there was no way the line was going to be cut out.

'We might have to write off half the royalties, but fuck it!' he said at the time. 'For someone in a suit to come along and say we've got to change a song we've been playing for two years isn't on.'

However, when 'Shakermaker' came out, it didn't feature the line, even if the tune itself was still uncomfortably similar to The New Seekers original, Liam howling 'I'd like to be somebody else and not know where I've been' so that it scanned to fit in with the original Coke theme.

Bonehead in yet another sumptuous gig location

Not that any of this mattered much, as 'Shakermaker' remains easily Oasis' weakest single to date, and no amount of petty musical larceny could hide the fact that this was a song in search of a decent chord progression, a hackneyed riff only brightened up by daft lyrical references to various characters such as Mr Soft, Mr Clean and Mr Ben who, according to the first verse, were living in Noel's loft. Or something.

As for the extra tracks, 'D'Yer Wanna be A Spaceman?' was a wafer-thin slice of acoustic whimsy, 'Alive' (an 8-track demo) was another crude rocker, while 'Bring It On Down' was a live version of a blistering song that sounded tinny and tame after translation onto vinyl/CD.

And yet, such was the force of the hype machine by this point in the Oasis saga that 'Shakermaker' couldn't fail to crashland into the upper reaches of the charts, which it did, entering in its first week at Number 11. That meant two-out-of-two hits so far.

It also meant Oasis could make their debut appearance on *Top Of The Pops*, a performance which certainly made up for the relatively disappointing music and which, for sheer alien delinquent cheek, almost ranked alongside Nirvana's *TOTP* appearance for 'Smells Like Teen Spirit', The Smiths for 'This Charming Man' and The Associates for 'Party Fears Two'.

The single's success chart-wise was undoubtedly helped by a ludicrously effusive Single Of The Week review in *Melody Maker* by Paul Mathur that described 'Shakermaker' as 'one of the hundred greatest songs ever written'.

As I say, ludicrous.

Oasis in Liverpool, April 1994

★★★★★★★ ★★★★★★★

'Live Forever'
'I just want to fly'

oasis

The Face rechristens the band 'The Sex Beatles' as Oasismania sweeps Britain . . . Oasis play their first festival – Glastonbury . . . Noel jams with Crazy Horse . . . and more bad boy behaviour at the Columbia hotel . . . Oasis hit America's New Music Seminar

SUMMER MADNESS

OASIS kept themselves busy during the first few months of summer '94, playing live, appearing at various festivals, jet-setting, being interviewed by every magazine under and over the sun (style Bible *The Face* put Oasis on the cover with the line: 'Never Mind The Bollocks, Here's The Sex Beatles'!!), and generally maintaining their reputation as pop's latest angels with dirty faces, getting into and out of more scrapes than most bands manage in a lifetime.

Oasis went on their first, sell-out headline tour in May, while Noel and Bonehead performed at 'Undrugged', Creation Records' 10th anniversary concert at the Royal Albert Hall, playing the band's forthcoming single 'Live Forever' as well as a primitive early version of 'Whatever'.

Then, in June, they made their festival debut at Glastonbury.

'Are you gonna wake up, then, for some real songs?' Liam goaded the sun-kissed, zonked-out, crusty student masses upon taking the stage. The band stormed through nine songs, including an encore of 'I Am The Walrus', to an ecstatic reaction. Excerpts from their festival performance were shown on Channel 4's *4 Goes To Glastonbury*.

Oasis', or at least Noel's, peak live moment surely came three days earlier, however, when he joined the ex-Icicle Works (the Liverpool band who had a hit 10 years before with 'Love Is A Wonderful Colour') frontman Ian McNabb onstage at London's King's College. McNabb was playing that night with Ralph Molina and Billy Talbot of Crazy Horse, the legendary cohorts of grizzly old rocker Neil Young.

Noel, a huge fan of Young and Crazy Horse, leapt at the chance to play alongside his heroes, and the foursome proceeded to rampage through a rousing version of 'Pushin' Too Hard' by original Sixties punks Sky Saxon And The Seeds, as well as a snatch of 'Rescue' by post-punk Liverpudlians Echo & The Bunnymen. (The brief King's College set was taped, and may well be issued at some point in 1995.) Crazy Horse themselves were so impressed with

Oasis wake up the blissed-out hordes, Glastonbury '94

Oasis unplugged at 'Undrugged', June 1994

Gallagher's impromptu jamming abilities that they travelled all the way to Manchester to see Oasis play live a few days later.

A euphoric Noel beamed, 'My mum's dead proud of me. I've had my picture taken with Arthur Lee [of Love], I've been onstage with Crazy Horse and I'm going to have my picture taken with Johnny Cash. All I need now is my picture taken with Burt Bacharach and I've got the full set!'

On a more serious note, he said of his jam with Crazy Horse: 'We're already respected by bands from the Sixties. We're respected by Paul Weller. You won't see Thom from fucking Radiohead playing with the Velvet fucking Underground or whatever.'

All of this furious activity must have gone to Noel and co's heads, because the night after Glastonbury the band got into a whole heap of mischief at legendary rock'n'roll hotel, the Columbia, in West London. By the band's own account, they got seriously drunk and, to cut a long story short, 'Things went out windows . . . we trashed the place.'

Elaborated Liam: 'They put us in the Columbia and at first it was a buzz being there. But then I thought it was a dive. There was a bug in the corner of my room and I thought, You can fuck off, this is my room. We had enough in the end. There was a lot of pot going round and we'd got some pipes. We were drinking as well and in the end we just trashed it. Then we started running round the place and going for it.'

The Columbia reacted by doing what they had only done twice before in their illustrious rock'n'roll history, to The Fall and The Mission: they banned Oasis.

The *Guardian* newspaper, obviously feeling this to be a high (or rather low) point in the celebrated history of rock'n'roll uncivil disobedience, an epoch-making incident on a par with The Rolling Stones urinating against a garage wall and The Beatles spliffing up in the bogs of Buckingham Palace after getting their OBEs, ran a two-pager detailing three decades of bad r'n'r behaviour in response to Oasis' laddish antics, antics which apparently involved – merciful heavens! – throwing their shoes around the hotel bar.

Oasis themselves were unrepentant. Said the Mancunian miscreants afterwards: 'Fuck 'em, we don't care. There's better hotels. It was the sort of place your Gran would have stayed in anyway.'

FOREVER PEOPLE

AT the end of July, Oasis played Tennants' 'T In the Park' Festival in Strathyclyde's Country Park, before heading off to Sweden to play the Hultsfred Festival.

High spirited as per usual, and assisted this time by their equally lively festival-mates Primal Scream and Verve (the latter are one of the few contemporary British groups whose music Oasis actually like), Oasis made front page news in the national press with some by-now-obligatory on-the-road shenanigans involving the smashing up of yet another hotel bar.

Backstage at Glastonbury

Let's raise one for America, July '94

'Hello, Room Trashing Incorporated – can I help you?'

Oasis: re-born in the USA

Liam recalls the event: 'I was walking along and this chair came flying past me. Then another, then another. I thought, It's gonna be good tonight. Primal Scream took off because we were getting a bit rowdy. They booked out at about two in the morning after we'd just smashed the place up – ripped the phones out and threw 'em out the window. We got arrested and banned from Sweden, and Primal Scream got off, the cunts.' Both Oasis and Verve were forced to pay nearly £1,000 in damages to the manager of the hotel, and, contrary to Liam's account, just managed to escape arrest after the police were called. To add injury to insult, Liam broke his foot while jumping off the tour bus the next day.

Before that little lot went off, though, Oasis had continent-hopped all the way to the States along with the cream of 1994's Britpack – Echobelly, These Animal Men, S*M*A*S*H, The Orb and Kaliphz – to play New York's annual industry round-up of new talent, the New Music Seminar.

The band were shadowed every step of the way by *Melody Maker*'s intrepid Paul Mathur. First he accompanied them to their American debut at Wetlands on 21st July (where they were sandwiched between Lotion and X-CNN), a performance subsequently described by Mathur in the paper as 'one of the best sets I've ever seen them play, Liam's [Johnny] Rottenesque sneer honed to perfection, Noel sublimely transcendent on guitar, the band just KNOWING they've got it exactly right.'

Mathur also listened in as the band blabbed their way through as many exclamatory claims ('We never, ever had any doubt that all of this would happen'; 'We're more important than some stupid industry circus') and defamatory put-downs (Liam on the shotgun suicide of Kurt Cobain: 'Don't talk to me about Nirvana. He was just a sad cunt who couldn't handle the fame. We're stronger than that. And you can fuck your fucking Pearl Jam as well') as they could squeeze into seven days.

Oasis tune up, Stateside

Finally, the '*Maker* journalist watched as the band filmed the video for their next single, 'Live Forever', in New York's Central Park. Liam really wanted to make the most of the opportunity and turn the event into an impromptu open-air gig by hiring a PA, but Noel flatly refused.

'Elvis Presley doesn't want to do it,' whinged Liam about his elder brother in a now familiar display of fraternal animosity. 'That's why he's a cunt and I hate him.'

There may have been no last-minute concert for the benefit of the tramps who roam Manhattan's most famous bit of greenery, but the video did get made in time for the release of the third Oasis single on August 8th, the week *Melody Maker* and *NME* broke tradition and both put the band on the front cover (it was, in fact, the first time the two 'inkies' had featured the same cover stars since U2 broke their silence in 1988 – apart from news coverage of the death of Kurt Cobain, of course) and 25 years to the day since The Beatles' renowned 'Abbey Road' zebra crossing LP shoot. The latter may or may not explain why the sleeve of 'Live Forever' featured a photo of the house where John Lennon grew up.

Like their first two singles, 'Live Forever' was backed with an acoustic number ('Up In The Sky', later electrified for the 'Definitely Maybe' album) and live track ('Supersonic', recorded in concert in April '94), as well as a song called 'Cloudburst', a hard'n'heavy chunk of psychedelic rock.

On their own, these three tracks would have made for a reasonably rewarding EP. However, 'Live Forever', of all the Oasis singles to date, was the one that least required any additives. A soaring anthem with a majestic chord progression courtesy of Noel and a deliciously plaintive vocal performance from Liam, 'Live Forever' is a glorious celebration of the potency of positive thinking and the absolute,

Trouble afoot – Liam gets pushed around in the States

unadulterated feeling of total possibility that is the natural right of the very beautiful and the very young.

'Live Forever' remains one of the best singles to be released this decade and was, along with Blur's 'Girls & Boys', by far the finest single of 1994. It was the record that cut the crap, the one that finally proved Oasis were more than just Manc motormouths with a cabal of overenthusiastic supporters in the media and an overweening sense of their own importance. Moreover, it was the record that suggested that here was a band destined for at least some of the greatness they believed to be their birthright.

As Noel told the *Melody Maker*, 'There's more to us than rumours, hearsay, gossip and sensationalism about drugs and fucking shagging in hotel rooms. This is what we're all about – songs. We're a real band with real songs and everything else is just incidental. That's what we'll be remembered for in 20 years' time, not incidents on ferries or drug busts or whatever.'

'Live Forever' was, basically, a classic. And it got to Number 10; Number One would have been about right.

★★★★★☆☆ ☆★★★★★★

'Definitely Maybe'
'Give it all you've got'

Oasis' 'Definitely Maybe' enters the British album charts at Number One . . . beating the popular operatics of the Three Tenors, it becomes the fastest selling debut LP of all time . . . Evan Dando of The Lemonheads jams with the marvels from Manchester at Virgin Records, Marble Arch . . .

RECORD BREAKERS

EVEN after scrapping entire sessions and using as many as seven – count 'em – studios, Oasis' debut album 'Definitely Maybe' still only cost a very modest £75,000. It was eventually produced by Noel Gallagher's mate from his Inspirals days, Mark Coyle, and Noel himself, while Electronic's producer Owen Morris was responsible for additional production, mastering and mixing chores.

Thanks to a colossal amount of pre-release press and the sort of buzz the industry definitely hadn't heard since the week before Suede's debut LP came out in 1993, maybe even since the release of the first Frankie Goes To Hollywood album in 1984, advance orders for 'Definitely Maybe' reached an unprecedented level.

As for the week it actually came out, there were yet more records broken. 'Definitely Maybe' first hit the shops on Tuesday August 30th (records are normally released on a

Liam and Noel plus friend (Evan Dando!) at Virgin Marble Arch

Monday, but that week it was a Bank Holiday). Within a few days, it had apparently sold about 150,000 copies, making it the fastest-selling debut album of the Nineties, as well as, arguably, the biggest-selling debut album of all time.

Needless to say, it entered the album charts at Number One, one place ahead of 'The Three Tenors' LP by globally famous

opera singers José Carreras, Placido Domingo and Luciano Pavarotti, a record which had been expected to sail to pole position given their huge across-the-board popularity as well as a television advertising campaign costing an estimated £2 million. Some reports stated that 'Definitely Maybe' actually sold between 10 and 20,000 more copies in its first week of release than 'The Three Tenors'. A spokesman for Creation Records – who, after ten years' releasing singles and albums, were now enjoying their very first Number One in any chart (they came very close with Primal Scream's 'Give Out But Don't Give Up' LP, which reached Number Two, and Sugar's 'Beaster' album [at Number Three]) – wryly commented: 'Three fat blokes shouting are no competition for Oasis.'

As for Oasis themselves, a spokesman for the band said: 'They love it. They say, "We're mad for it." They want to be the biggest band. There's no point settling for anything less. You've gotta have ambition.'

The very same day 'Definitely Maybe' was released, 1,000 Oasis fans turned up at the Marble Arch branch of Virgin Megastore to see their favourite band perform an impromptu acoustic, *Unplugged*-style selection of tracks from the album. Unfortunately, although Virgin have an entertainments licence from Westminster City Council, they are limited to a 200 capacity, so, when the band started playing, only a small number of their devotees were allowed in to watch.

Eventually, Oasis ran through their three hit singles, as well as 'Sad Song' (an extra track only available on the vinyl version of the album) and 'Slide Away'.

And then, as they prepared to play future Christmas smash 'Whatever', they were joined by Sultan of Slacker, Evan Dando of The Lemonheads, who proceeded to rattle a tambourine and add backing vocals to the song! After the brief show, Dando explained to *Melody Maker* how he had become Noel Gallagher's mate as well as Oasis' biggest fan.

'We met about a month ago and hit it off,' said the flaxen-haired indie pin-up. 'Then, last night, we collided in Paris. We'd both been playing the Lowlands festival in Holland and we wrote a song together called "Purple Parallelogram".

'I really like Oasis' lack of pretension,' he added, 'but I won't be signing any autographs today because that would be impolite. This is their day.'

Indeed it was.

'Definitely Maybe' has subsequently sold almost half-a-million copies in the UK – making it a platinum album – as well as thousands more overseas.

Not bad for a first shot.

CERTAINLY . . . PROBABLY

BUT was it any good?

Definitely! Maybe . . .

One couldn't help but have at least some reservations about the band's debut album. First of all, on a purely value-for-money basis, there were only five tracks diehard Oasis fans wouldn't have owned before (and they would probably have heard those live) – 'Rock'N'Roll Star', 'Cigarettes & Alcohol' (which was due to be the band's fourth single anyway), 'Digsy's Dinner', 'Slide Away' and 'Married With Children' – or six if you happened to buy the vinyl version of 'Definitely Maybe', because it contained the previously unavailable 'Sad Song'.

And secondly, notwithstanding the excellence of much of the material, there was a definite whiff of déja vu about the whole project due in no small part to Oasis' stubborn insistence on the conventional four-square rock band line-up of guitar, bass, drums and vocals. Suffice it to say that none of the tracks would have jarred had they been aired in '84, '74 or, indeed, 1964.

Not only that, but you would have been hard pressed to squeeze all the obvious steals and examples of creative pilfering into a three-volume book. You didn't need to be an anorak-clad obsessive with an encyclopaedic knowledge of rock history to spot all the T-Rex, Sex Pistols, Stone Roses,

Beatles, Rolling Stones, Happy Mondays, Kinks, David Bowie, Small Faces, Faces, Neil Young, Jam and Who musical references liberally sprinkled all over the (mainly CD) 'grooves' of 'Definitely Maybe'.

In fact, some tracks were virtually replicas of ancient material. 'Digsy's Dinner', to cite one example, had such a similar riff to 'Lazy Sunday' by The Small Faces it was a surprise writs weren't issued within days of 'Definitely Maybe' coming out. And 'Cigarettes & Alcohol' was so like T-Rex's 'Get It On', it's a wonder poor old Marc Bolan hasn't dug his way out of his Bushey grave to wreak posthumous revenge on the outrageously cheeky Noel Gallagher.

But perhaps all this was missing the point somewhat. Because, as I myself pointed out in my review of the album in the August 27th issue of *Melody Maker*, 'You shouldn't expect samples, sequencers, dance beats or any other concessions to late-20th century pop life here. Nor should you anticipate any idiosyncratic curlicues or strange experiments in sound. Fuck that – that's what The Prodigy, Orbital and The Aphex Twin are for. Oasis have been called retro – you can fuck that as well.

'In no other sphere of human activity than pop music,' I ranted on (and on), 'do we apply such rigorous attention to originality of intent or achievement. Do we turn off 'The Bill' because it's not as good as 'The Sweeney'? Do we chuck out our dinner because it doesn't taste as good as something we ate back in the Eighties?! Do we fuck - no, we surrender to the gloriously vivid immediacy of the moment.'

BACK-TRACKING

THE above attitude certainly helped overcome any misgivings I, or anyone else for that matter, may have had about the sometimes absurdly familiar nature of Oasis' trad-rock attack.

Besides, once you'd managed to get over the LP material's lack of originality, you were free to enjoy what was nearly one hour's worth of good, old-fashioned, brash, electric, energetic rock'n'roll. If nothing else, like 'Suede' (in hock to David Bowie up to its elbows), 'The Stone Roses' (ditto, only for Bowie read The Byrds) and Teenage Fanclub's 'Bandwagonesque' (Big Star) before it, 'Definitely Maybe' proves that, as far as rock'n'roll is concerned, the future may well be just a tad overrated.

Or, as Paul Mathur beautifully put it, 'Eleven tracks, each a potential single, and the whole a fully-formed, power chord-drenched justification for why guitar music can rape the senses.'

Exactly.

Oasis rock the Astoria, August '94

As an LP-opener, 'Rock'N'Roll Star' was fantastically exciting, an inspiring paean to the power of the imagination and arguably the most explosive introduction to any album since 'The Headmaster Ritual' kickstarted The Smiths' 'Meat Is Murder'. 'Shakermaker' and 'Live Forever', the next two songs, were untouched in their transition from single to album. 'Up In The Sky' was a ferociously amped-up version of the track that originally appeared on the B-side of the 'Live Forever' single. 'Columbia' was as wild, wired and weird as ever, a terrace chant in search of a football match.

Then came 'Supersonic', as snottily infectious as ever ('You can have it all but how much do you want it?'). 'Bring It Down' was a raw guitar rampage worthy of the Pistols or The Stooges that managed to sound even more live than the live version previously available on the flip of 'Shakermaker'. 'Cigarettes & Alcohol' was another example of Noel Gallagher's genius for writing obscenely simple three-chord wonders that, after one play, you feel like

you've heard a zillion times — the mark of a great pop songwriter, that.

'Cigarettes & Alcohol' also demonstrated once more Noel's knack for coming up with naggingly memorable lyrics-cum-catchphrases ('You gotta make it happen!') as well as sneaky drug references ('You might as well do the white line'). If that wasn't enough, the track featured some superbly sneery Johnny Rottenish vowel/consonant extensions from brother Liam ('Is it myyyy imaginayyy-sheee-yunnn?) After that, 'Digsy's Dinner' was, as I've said, just a throwaway little jaunt down memory lane, one marked 'Steve Marriot'.

The 10th track, called 'Slide Away', was something else entirely, however. Over a gorgeously melancholy series of minor chords and some exquisite guitar patterns reminiscent of Neil Young circa 'Cortez The Killer' or 'Like A Hurricane', Liam, clearly singing on Noel's behalf (the latter split with his longterm girlfriend in 1994), mourned the loss of the love of his life ('I dream of you, and all the things you say/I wonder

where you are now . . .') while at the same time imagining the prospect of escaping dull reality with either the same, or another, girl of his fantasies ('Slide in, baby — together we'll fly'). Lovely.

After the orgasm, the anti-climax: 'Married With Children', a lighthearted acoustic anecdote (rock music should never, ever, be lighthearted), again obviously about Noel, and an ex-girlfriend who keeps moaning at him for playing crap music and keeping her awake at night with same. Very nice, in a Gerry & The Pacemakers sort of way. If you like that sort of thing.

'Sad Song' more than made up for 'Married With Children' (if you bought 'Definitely Maybe' on vinyl, that is), a gently pretty acoustic lament for lost love — yet again! — that suggested there was rather more to Noel Gallagher than just smashing up hotel bar furniture and defenestrating television sets.

As he told the NME's John Harris, 'I'm a lover, not a fighter.'

Hey!

Paul Weller's favourite new guitarist, Noel Gallagher

Oasis: better than Pavarotti, apparently

★★★★★☆☆ ☆★★★★★★

'Cigarettes & Alcohol'
'You gotta make it happen!'

oasis

Top, Oasis hit Nagoya, Japan. Bottom, the fans in Dublin refuse to go home.

WHAT THE PAPERS SAID

THE reviews of 'Definitely Maybe' were almost universally ecstastic. Of the music weeklies, *NME* gave it an impressive 9/10 and said it was like 'opening your bedroom curtains one morning and discovering that some fucker's built the Taj Mahal in your back garden and then filled it with your favourite flavour of Angel Delight', which I'm sure meant something to the journalist when he wrote it; and *Melody Maker* called it 'a record full of songs to live by, made by a gang of reckless northern reprobates – yeah, we hacks love a bit of rough – who you can easily dream of joining.'

The monthlies were no less keen on the album. *Mojo* praised its 'spunky, adolescent rock'. *Q* called the album 'a riot . . . manna from heaven'. *Vox* correctly noted that Oasis 'have a faultless pedigree that includes every great British rock'n'roll band of the last 30

The album receives unanimously rave reviews in all sections of the press . . . despite it being the fourth single off the album, 'Cigarettes And Alcohol' gets to Number Seven . . . there is rising tension during the band's American tour, some shows being cancelled . . . and Noel Gallagher gets punched in Newcastle . . .

'Heil Oasis!' – Tokyo, September 1994

Noel jams with the Japanese Beatles

years'. And *Select*, awarding it five-out-of-five stars, decided that 'whatever The Stone Roses are doing out in Wales [the other great Manchester band of the last half decade or so had yet to release their long-awaited second album], they may as well pack up and go home'.

Even dance magazine *Mixmag*, who rarely if ever review guitar-based records, gave 'Definitely Maybe' 10/10 and concluded: 'If you're into music, be it techno, hip hop, jungle or classic hands-towards-the-ceiling pumping house, you could still get into this.'

Then there were the dailies – specifically the 'serious' broadsheets – normally less prone to dizzy hyperbole. The *Independent* commented: 'The UK can still be relied upon to throw up a classic world-beating guitar band every few years. Oasis are the best for some time.' The *Daily Telegraph* homed in on Oasis' 'jangly, swaggering pop songs and snappy, arrogant lyrics'. The *Guardian*

Noel and Liam: the brothers grim

The 'I Am The Walrus' sequence from the Beatles' *Magical Mystery Tour*

celebrated its 'guitar pop, distilled to its simplest, most infectious form, without ambiguity or gender confusion'. And *The Times* reckoned that, 'As an uncomplicated celebration of youthful brio, this is an album which takes some beating.'

In fact across the journalistic board, only David Cheal, offering a second opinion in the *Daily Telegraph*, had a less than kind word to say about Oasis at this point, making the comment: 'They have about as much chance of becoming the new Beatles as Dannii

Minogue has of becoming the new Diana Ross; they simply do not belong on the same musical planet, and catchy though songs like "Supersonic" and "Live Forever" may be, they are hardly likely to become ingrained in the very fabric of our culture . . .

'No,' he summed up, 'Oasis may not be the new Beatles, but with their gift for memorable hooks, their guitar-dominated sound and their penchant for meaningless lyrics, they could be the new Slade.' Bitch.

BEER WE GO AGAIN

THE general public clearly didn't give a fig about original this or Beatles that, because, when 'Cigarettes & Alcohol', the band's fourth single and the fourth to be lifted from 'Definitely Maybe', was released in October, it was bought by more people than any of their previous singles, entering the charts at a highly impressive Number Seven.

The success of 'Cigarettes & Alcohol' was doubly pleasing because it suggested that Oasis were doing what no other 'indie' band apart from Blur in recent years has done, and achieve that all-important crossover from critical faves to student raves to join that rare group reserved for the select few in the upper echelons of the Rock Stratosphere known simply as The People's Choice.

The sleeve of the single, with its carefully contrived shot of Oasis 'spontaneously' enjoying themselves and partying with various mates and girls and cigarettes and alcohol, indicated what we already suspected – that this was debauched and depraved business as usual.

Apart from the title track, the EP featured a ragged version of 'I Am The Walrus' recorded live in Glasgow in June '94, as well as the previously unreleased 'Listen Up' and 'Fade Away'. 'Listen Up' was arguably the best extra track yet offered free on their four EPs, a strident rock ballad with an affecting chord sequence all about how 'One fine day I'm gonna leave you all behind' (many of Noel Gallagher's lyrics are about escape to a better world – a rock star world?), while 'Fade Away' was a blistering rocker along the lines of 'Rock'N'Roll Star'. Good stuff.

DEFINITELY MAYHEM

IT wasn't all good news during late summer and early autumn '94, however. In October, the *NME* ran a live review from the band's American tour at Los Angeles' Whiskey-A-

Two Japanese fans clearly in awe of 'The Brothers'

Go-Go entitled 'Definitely Mayhem' that indicated all was not well in the Oasis camp, pinpointing the shambolic nature of their performance, as well as the tension between audience and band.

The same week, there was a news story suggesting 'Oasis' future was temporarily in doubt after rumours that Noel Gallagher had left the band following a furious row with brother Liam during their American tour.'

Noel's 'disappearance' meant Oasis were forced to cancel shows in Austin, Dallas, Kansas and Missouri. A US spokesman for the band offered 'band fatigue' as the official reason for the cancellations.

There was even worse crowd-band rivalry back home two months before when Noel was attacked onstage by an audience member during Oasis' set at Newcastle's Riverside on August 9th. Tension had gathered all evening with football chants such as 'Man City, wank wank wank' (Oasis love Man City) and 'Soft as shite' being directed at the group.

At first, Noel couldn't work out why things blew up that night in the way they did and the stranger attacked him, he just said: 'We didn't stop and ask him, we just kicked his fuckin' arse, threw him outside and went backstage. I had blood all over the place, there was no way I was going back. My guitar was trashed anyway cos I hit the cunt on the back of the head with it.

'We had to drive out that gig down a sidestreet with three hundred people lined up along the pavement,' he continued, 'and they just smashed the van to bits. Why play for a load of fuckin' monkeys, man? Hopefully all this'll pass.'

Later on, however, Noel put the incident down to the aggressive nature of the song they were playing at the time, 'Bring It Down'.

'It incites violence,' he said. 'That song and "Fade Away" are the two punk songs in the set, and it always gets pretty hairy when we play them. But I never thought it would come to somebody standing up onstage and giving me a black eye.

'There was no forewarning,' he went on. 'Usually you'll get one person in the audience who'll stand there and call you a wanker all night. But this was the first gig in a long time where that hadn't happened. Nothing had been thrown onstage and nobody had spat at us. The next thing we know, I've got this massive cut down the side of my face! I didn't realise that I'd been cut until someone gave me this wet towel and said, "You'd better put that on your eye". I said, "Why?" Then I looked at my shirt and there was blood all over it.'

Assessing the band's growing Mancunian hard-nut reputation later on that night, Noel Gallagher said: 'We're not about fighting, we just want to play our songs. But if someone gets up and thinks he's hard, then he's going to get it.'

The following morning, the *Daily Mirror* reacted with typically magnificent tabloid calm to the incident.

Fret it be!

'Oasis sunk by fans' bloodbath!' screamed the headline of their story, going on: 'Top rockers Oasis were forced to cancel a sell-out show in Newcastle amid an orgy of violence.'

The rival *Daily Star* picked up the baton when, in a two-page feature imaginatively entitled 'SEX'N'DRUGS'N'ROCK'N'ROLL', they ran a detailed portrayal of Oasis as 'The Frightening Five'.

'They're the wildest and most outrageous rock band since The Who launched their notorious orgies of mayhem and destruction,' frothed the *Daily Star*'s John Poole, a man who clearly hasn't been out much these past few decades. 'Shattered hotel rooms, bloody brawls, drugs and groupies are all part of everyday life for these Manchester council estate toughies.

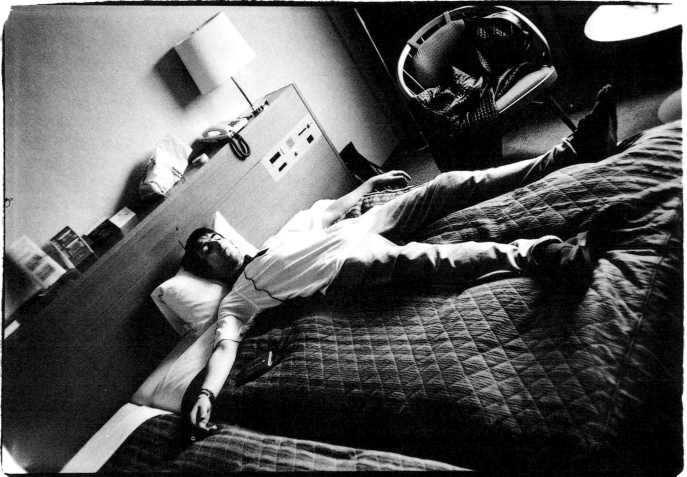

Top, Oasis in Osaka, Japan, September '94. Bottom, in bed with Liam, Nagoya, Japan

Noel grabs a root beer on Route 95, New Jersey

★★★★★★ ★★★★★★

'Whatever'
'I'm free to be whatever I choose'

'Oi, you! Outside – now!' Liam takes on Brighton, December '94

America, less eager to embrace Britain's Next Big Things, respond to Oasis . . . Japan treat the band like they are the new Beatles . . . 'Whatever' narrowly misses the Christmas Number One slot . . . Oasis win numerous awards at the end of the year, and Best Newcomers at Brits '95 . . .

Cambridge, December '94

FOREIGN AFFAIRS

HAVING established themselves as the best new band in Britain, Oasis spent the latter half of 1994 proving they were no parochial UK hype.

First, they consolidated their summer US success, a continent whose music-listening public has, over the years, learned to be suspicious of any Next Big Thing from England, the latter a country with a reputation for, as the cliché goes, building 'em up and knocking 'em down, often managing both within the short space of twelve months.

It was this natural supicion that led to dismal attempts to Make It Big Stateside over the the last decade by the likes of Frankie Goes To Hollywood, The Smiths, The Stone Roses, Happy Mondays and Suede, and the signs were that Oasis would have equal difficulty convincing the relatively conservative American press and public that they were more than just another fey and faddish 'British Haircut Band'.

A typical example of sceptical American press appeared in the *Los Angeles Times* in September: 'Oasis are just another perfectly gratifying but fairly mediocre pop outfit with fab sunglasses and mod hairdos.'

Noel Gallagher had a theory as to why Oasis were going to crack the States, as opposed to, say, Blur or Suede, who were too Anglocentric, even Londoncentric, what with all their preoccupations with going down the dog tracks at Walthamstow (Blur) or eccentric, sexually ambiguous songs about pantomime horses (Suede), whereas Oasis addressed more universal concerns, to whit: Sex, Drugs, Cigarettes, Alcohol, Youth, Relationships, Marriage, Boredom, Freedom, Rebellion and Rock'N'Roll.

This writer had his own (brilliantly original) theory regarding the likelihood of Oasis appealing to America, one that I expressed in an interview with the *Washington Post* in October.

'Traditionally,' I pontificated to the *Post* journalist (actually *MM*'s own Paul Mathur using a pseudonym!), in my official capacity as *Melody Maker* Features Editor and therefore Person Very Slightly Responsible For Breaking Oasis, 'American bands are only ever any good at rock, while British groups are better at pop – and America doesn't really like pop. Unlike the very poppy Blur and Suede – not an ounce of rock in their bodies – Oasis are well-placed because their music lies exactly at the halfway point between rock and pop. That will ensure their music will be enjoyed by yer average American rock fan.'

Actually, it is probably too early to say whether or not Oasis are going to go supernova U2-style in the States - America is far bigger and, therefore, takes far longer to submit to new sensations than Britain - but the fact is that 'Definitely Maybe' has sold many, many thousands of copies Stateside.

Then there's Japan.

Japan took approximately five minutes to submit to Oasis'. charms. Mens magazine *GQ* followed the band to Tokyo in September '94 and discovered that, for today's young Japanese, Oasis are the new Fab Four.

'As the Oasis tour bus noses its way out of traffic into a neon-lit side street, an ear-splitting shriek, louder than a wail of feedback, rips through the air,' wrote *GQ* journalist Daniela Soave. 'Hundreds of girls hurtle towards the vehicle, pounding on its windows, rocking it from side to side . . . Oasis have provoked mass hysteria in the normally restrained Japanese fans. I could be witnessing the second coming.'

Southampton, November 1994

Liam Gallagher: the frontman . . .

. . .with the most front

OH WELL, WHATEVER

IN December 1994, the words 'inexorable' and 'rise' kept springing to mind whenever the subject of Oasis cropped up. Because that was the month Oasis enjoyed their fifth hit single in nine months, with a record that only missed being the Christmas Number One by two places, thanks to a bunch of bum-fluffed saccharine rappers from Walthamstow called East 17 and a lachrymose Yuletide ballad screeched by a chubby-faced American harridan called Mariah Carey.

'Whatever', the single in question and the first not to be lifted from 'Definitely Maybe', also only just narrowly missed being the second Oasis record to cause a major legal rumpus in nine months. Because – and this is apart from the public uproar caused by the fact that 'Whatever' sounds more like The Beatles than The Beatles – early copies of the song that did the rounds during the last couple of months of '94 featured a line that went 'All the young blues' and bore such a remarkable melodic resemblance to Mott The Hoople's 'All The Young Dudes' that David Bowie, composer of '. . . Dudes', was rumoured to be threatening to sue Oasis.

When 'Whatever' did come out, on December 19th – timed to perfection to coincide with the last singles chart of the year, the one traditionally known as 'The

Guigsy gives it some bass

Oasis perform 'Shakermaker' on *Top Of The Pops*, June '94

Noel on the video set for 'Whatever'

Christmas Chart' – the 'offending' line had been removed, nixing the band's chances of being involved in a protracted courtroom wrangle with David Bowie. Shame.

The single, described by Noel Gallagher earlier in the year as 'the greatest song ever written' (and only he knows how close his tongue was to his cheek at the time), did, however, reach Number Three in the charts, an especially impressive feat considering the competitive nature of the Top 40 at that time of year. 'Whatever' has since sold in excess of 200,000 copies and is, at the time of writing (early February), still in the Top 20, further proof that Oasis have Crossed Over (singles by 'indie' bands usually enter the charts for one week only to disappear without trace the following week after all the hardcore fans have bought them).

Apart from its affecting 'Abbey Road'-era strings and singalongachorus as well as the obligatory Single Of The Week accolades in *NME* ('The best single of 1994') and *MM* ('Single Of The Fuckin' Year, mate'), the success of 'Whatever' was also helped by Oasis performing it on *Later With Jools Holland*, a TV appearance that surely endeared the band to fortysomething rockers in viewerland who hadn't heard a new record for years but wanted something that took them back to the halcyon days of The Beatles and the Stones.

The extra tracks on the EP couldn't have done much harm, either, not least because at least one of them, '(It's Good) To Be Free', was almost up there with 'Slide Away' for sheer poignant rock ballad perfection. Coincidentally, 'Slide Away' was on the flip of 'Whatever', too, as was 'Half The World Away', yet another acoustic paean to

Backstage at *Top Of The Pops*, December '94

The Brats and the Brits: Oasis outside the NME 'Brats' event (top) at which they scooped three awards, and (bottom) being presented with the Best Newcomers award by Kink Ray Davies at the annual music industry Brits Awards, February '95

freedom and escape. Contrary to reports in the music press, the introspective, Kurt Cobain-if-he'd-gone-solo-ish 'Talk Tonight' (Liam: 'The one Noel wrote while he was in San Francisco with some fuckin' bird, that's shit and I fuckin' hate it') and 'Live By The Sea' (Liam: 'Dead heavy, that one Very good') were not on the 'Whatever' EP.

Oasis ended 1994 with a clutch of Best Album/Single/Band Of The Year awards from a huge cross-section of magazine writers, and they won a variety of categories in the *Melody Maker* readers' poll (including Lip Of The Year, for Liam, and Hype Of The Year for

the band). They also entered 1995 being nominated for several Brits as well as numerous Brats, the alternative awards ceremony organised by the *NME*. In the latter they topped the Readers' Poll for Best New Band and Best Single (Live Forever), and 'Definitely Maybe' was voted Album of the Year by *NME* journalists.

Then in February the band was recognised in the annual Brits awards, the flagship event for the British recording industry, trouncing their rivals in the Best Newcomers category.

So there you have it. Oasis: not just the best new band in Britain, but also the hardest new band in Britain.

Only bullets - or a bad record - can stop them now.

★★★★★★ ★★★★★★★★

'Wonderwall'
'Today is gonna be the day'

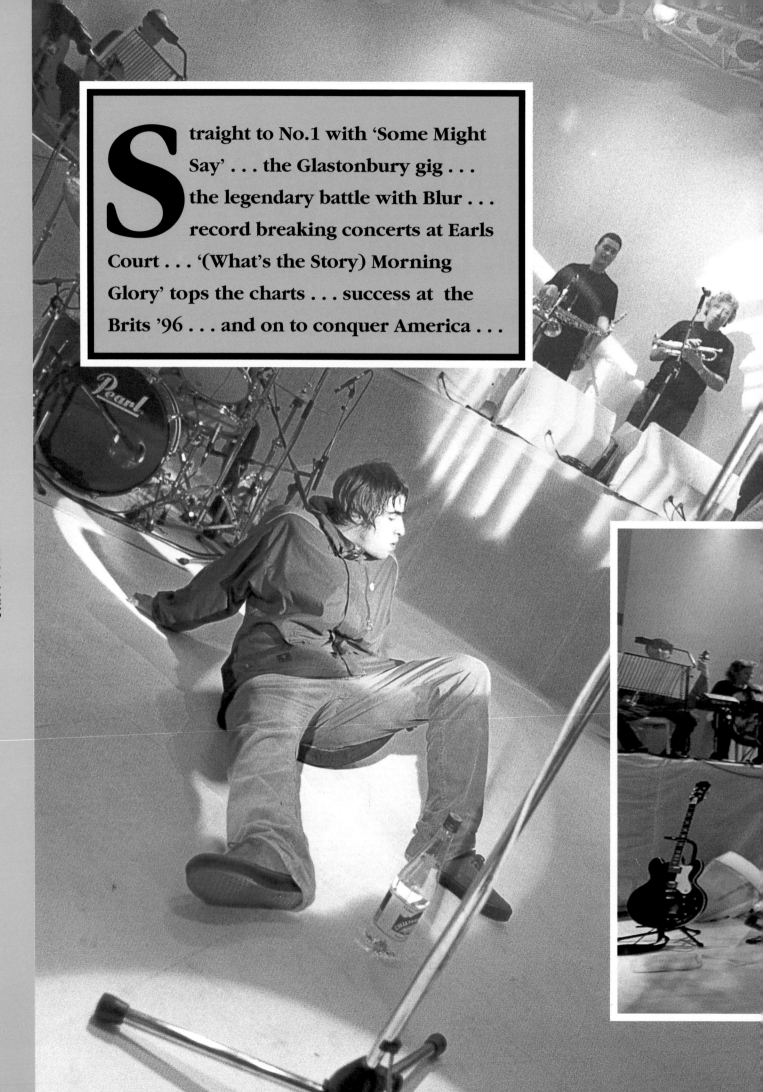

Straight to No.1 with 'Some Might Say' . . . the Glastonbury gig . . . the legendary battle with Blur . . . record breaking concerts at Earls Court . . . '(What's the Story) Morning Glory' tops the charts . . . success at the Brits '96 . . . and on to conquer America . . .

HE'S ELECTRIC

YOU could say that, despite having sold more than one million copies of 'Definitely Maybe', despite the five Top 40 hits and despite their growing status as Blur's only serious rivals in the Britpop stakes, for Oasis 1994 was just a dress rehearsal. You could say that. With some justification you could say that. As their Brit Award demonstrated, Oasis started 1995 as The Best New Band In Britain. By the start of 1996, their meteoric ascent in America meant they were about to become the biggest band on the planet. Most groups would gladly retire on what Oasis achieved in their first 12 months. But anyone who expected them to rest on their laurels clearly didn't understand what this particular group were about. And what they were about was total world domination. Otherwise, what was the point?

The key to Oasis' success lay, of course, in Noel Gallagher's songs and Liam Gallagher's attitude. Oasis' performance at the 1995 Brit Awards, a rendition of 'Don't Look Back In Anger', a new song from their second album, yet to be released, was just fine, the sort of beautiful, yearning ballad at which Gallagher Snr was becoming expert. But it was Liam's 'performance' as he pimp-rolled towards the stage, fag in hand, to collect the award that really stole the show. As he approached the steps, he effected a tiny, soft-sneaker shuffle to change direction. It was a shimmy that probably lasted about one millisecond, yet it was more graceful than a ballet dancer and more rock'n'roll than most band's careers. It was without doubt one of the most glorious pop moments of the past 10 years.

Liam Gallagher had, in no time at all, earned a reputation as the incendiary frontman of the Nineties. Yet his unpredictable onstage antics were no theatrical displays of macho braggadocio or fake live-wire intensity: he didn't just turn it off the minute the band's concerts came to an end. This might explain his mercurial behaviour around the world throughout Oasis' second year in the spotlight.

At the end of February, for example, after spending four hours downing double gin and tonics in Manchester's Dry bar, Liam allegedly got into a fight that culminated in him throwing around glasses and ashtrays, thowing up, being thrown out of the famous drinking emporium and getting into a further physical encounter with a cab driver.

'I live for now,' Liam said by way of explanation, 'not for what happens after I die. If I die and there's something afterwards, I'm going to hell, not heaven. I mean, the devil's got all the good gear. What's God got? The Inspiral Carpets and nuns. Fuck that.'

On the other hand, as *Melody Maker's* Paul Mathur attempted to demonstrate in an article in April, there was more to Liam than fucking and fighting.

'I'm going to change things this year,' the singer decided. 'I'm giving up the pot and

New drummer Alan White rolls with it

NUMBER ONE WITH A BULLET

McCARROLL'S replacement, Londoner Alan White, the 22-year-old younger brother of former Style Council drummer, Steve White, had a fairly auspicious debut public appearance to contend with: performing on *Top Of The Pops* for Oasis' electrifying live rendition of 'Some Might Say', their brilliant sixth single and very first Number One, which entered the charts at pole position in May.

In an exclusive interview with *Melody Maker* a few weeks before the release of 'Some Might Say', Noel Gallagher joked that, after borrowing heavily from The Beatles, T.Rex and Mott The Hoople for the previous few Oasis singles, this time he'd 'ripped off "Ooh La La" by The Faces.' Paul Mathur described the new single as like 'a combination of "Cigarettes And Alcohol" and "Live Forever",' while describing its lyrics as a cross between 'the enchanting gibberish' of 'Supersonic' and 'Shakermaker'.

'Basically,' Paul Mathur concluded, prescient as ever, 'it's everything they've ever done before honed into a sure-fire chart hit. And after you've heard it a couple of times, you'll remember it for decades. That's what classic pop's about.'

The *Melody Maker's* David Stubbs made it Single Of The Week and really rose to the occasion, calling Oasis 'simply magnificent, magnificently simple' and referring to 'Some Might Say' as 'single of the year by a white hot streak, a moment in the sky we can all share.'

He wasn't wrong: starting with a two-note guitar riff plucked straight from Noel Gallagher's mental jukebox, 'Some Might Say' was definately the kind of record old people always claim they used to make but don't any more, a 'Satisfaction' or 'Anarchy In The UK' for the post-rave generation, another effortless Oasis celebration of youth, pleasure and possibility based around the eternally stimulating bass/guitar/drums set-up.

Apart from the superb title cut, on the 'Some Might Say' EP, Oasis' ever generous songwriter offered three excellent extra

being pissed and lazy so much. I'm going to learn to play the guitar properly and try to do some writing.'

However, Liam wasn't going to turn over a new leaf just yet. In fact, there was more trouble in March, this time while Oasis were on tour in America. During a concert in Cleveland, Liam was forced to chide an insensitive audience for chucking coins at support act, and fellow Creation band, Velvet Crush – the latter's mainman, Ric Menck, suffered a gash on the forehead. Only days later, in Indianapolis, Liam himself was struck on the head by a pair of metal-frame glasses thrown from the crowd, which led Oasis to stop the gig after two songs.

There were fairly persistent reports of scraps between Liam and brother Noel throughout early '95, one of which culminated in Noel storming out of recording sessions for the second Oasis album. Liam even managed to get into a ruck with the lead singer of Menswear, the bright new hopes (some might say 'bright new clothes horses') of the Britpop scene, after one London gig.

More seriously still was the bloody punch-up in a topless Paris dive between Liam and drummer Tony McCarroll. It was hardly surprising when news stories emerged at the end of April, stating that McCarroll had left the band.

Oasis were about to eclipse their many 1994 achievements. Now all they had to do was keep the band together.

Liam and Noel party on at Glastonbury '95 with Robbie Williams

tracks: 'Talk Tonight', a bluesy acoustic ballad crooned affectingly by Noel which caught the tunesmith at the end of his tether in some far-flung hotel bedroom, feeling sad and lonely, and which sounded like Kurt Cobain 'Unplugged' and unhinged; 'Acquiesce' anticipated the sort of back-to-their-roots, primal screaming of R.E.M.'s 'Monster'; while 'Headshrinker' outdid the punkiest of the punks.

It seemed as though Noel could churn this stuff out in his sleep. Not that he would always want to, as he explained to Ted Kessler of *NME* on the eve of Oasis' headlining appearance at Glastonbury '95.

'I see it as three albums and that's it,' he said, casually dramatic. 'I don't think

I can do any more with Oasis after that. I think a band like us will have run our course after that. There's only so many anthems you can write. What will I do next? Sell shoes, probably.'

ON A ROLL'

NOEL wasn't about to leave Oasis and start working for Dolcis just yet. For starters, there was that Glastonbury appearance to be getting on with, which even dieheards – and the band themselves – felt was some what below par and lacklustre (afterwards, the consensus among the revellers was that the festival highlights were the performances by The Prodigy and Pulp).

Then there were the two special shows

that were to take place on a Scottish beach, at Irvine near Ayr, in mid-July - the band had one of the largest free-standing tents in existence specially shipped in from China for the gigs.

Oasis' next venture has since entered the record books under the section fairly tamely marked 'historic': the two biggest bands in Indiedom, Blur and Oasis, decided to release their brand new singles, respectively 'Country House' and 'Roll With It', on the same day – Monday, August 14th.

This was no less than an attempt on the part of both bands to 'have it out' in public, to find out once and for all who was the most popular group in a no-holds-barred race for the Number One slot, a real-life

Everybody who was anybody on Planet Pop saw the lads at Earls Court

Battle Of The Bands. Never in the history of pop – even during those early, mostly imaginary bids for commercial supremacy between The Beatles and The Rolling Stones, T Rex and Slade, The Sex Pistols and The Clash, The Stone Roses and Happy Mondays – had two bands actually gone out of their way to ensure the exact same release date for their records.

By Sunday, August 20th, the word was out: despite early reports that 'Roll With It' (backed with the acoustic 'It's Better People', which was a bit like Stephen Stills' 'Love The One You're With', the plaintive 'Rockin' Chair' and 'Live Forever', the latter recorded

September 1995 was no less busy for Oasis (and remember: the biggest 'alternative' band before Oasis were The Stone Roses, who only ever managed about one public act per year). They had their first-ever live video released, which was filmed during a seaside show at Southend Cliffs Pavilion earlier that year, in April. And their September tour of Britain sold out in half an hour - the special freephone number set up for the occasion was hit by about 35,000 calls in the 30 minutes after the tickets went on sale, causing the system to overload; some fans even started queueing outside venue box offices as early as 3am!

Unfortunately, many of the aforementioned dates had to be rescheduled for October/November due to the 'nervous exhaustion' (usually, although not in this instance, rockspeak for drug addiction) of bassist Paul McGuigan, who fell ill in mid-September.

'Look, I'm fuckin' shot to bits. I don't think I can get on a bus and go on tour,' a shattered McGuigan told his bandmates straight after recording sessions for Oasis' second LP and a tour of Japan.

'The poor lad just needs a bit of a lie down,' said Noel, quashing rumours that the band were about to split up. The songwriter, seemingly quite serious, also told the *Daily Mirror:* 'Paul is Oasis. If he leaves, the band is finished. It's that simple.'

McGuigan would be back with Oasis within a couple of months, just in time for their record-breaking concerts at Earl's Court in November. Meanwhile, the band ended one of their busiest months to date with two key stories, one involving an act of charity, the other revolving around a throwaway comment from Noel Gallagher that was far from charitable.

First, there was the 'War Child' project in aid of Bosnia – Oasis recorded a new version of 'Fade Away' with actor Johnny Depp on guitar, while Noel recorded a version of The Beatles' 'Come Together' with two of his all time heroes, Paul McCartney and Paul Weller (the track was later released as a single under the band name The Mojo Filters).

live at Glastonbury '95) was outselling 'Country House' by five copies to three, Blur entered the charts at Number One, with Oasis snapping at their heels at Number Two. Blur had won the first major skirmish in The Battle Of Britpop (although, as we soon found out, the war was far from over), 'Country House' just managing to outsell their rivals due to their then-larger teen and crossover audiences .

Secondly, there were the less altruistic, off-the-cuff remarks made by Noel about Blur in an interview with *The Observer*.

'The guitarist [Graham Coxon] I've got a lot of time for. The drummer I've never met – I hear he's a nice guy. The bass player and the singer – I hope the pair of them catch AIDS and die because I fucking hate them two.'

The tabloid press immediately snapped into action, feigning predictable outrage. As for the Oasis camp, there were hesitant promises to donate money to AIDS charities, as well as a letter written by Noel, which was sent directly to *Melody Maker*.

'I would like to apologise to all concerned who took offence at my comments about Damon Albarn and Alex James,' the letter started, Noel going on to offer an explananation for his ugly remarks: 'It must have been the fiftieth time that interview that I was pressed to give an opinion on Blur. As soon as I said it, I realised it was an insensitive thing to say as AIDS is no joking matter, and immediately retracted the comment, but was horrified to pick up *The Observer* and find the journalist concerned chose to still run with it.

'Anyone who knows me will confirm that I've always been sympathetic towards the plight of HIV carriers and AIDS sufferers,' Noel's letter continued, 'as well as being supportive of the challenge to raise awareness about AIDS and HIV.'

Noel ended the written apology: 'Although not being a fan of their music, I wish both Damon and Alex a long and healthy life.'

GLORY DAYS

FORTUNATELY, the release of the second Oasis album in October helped to remove the nasty taste of Noel's unusually offensive comments from people's mouths: '(What's The Story) Morning Glory?' was another fabulous collection of Gallagher anthems, albeit one that veered away from the celebratory tone of 'Definitely Maybe' towards a more mature, even melancholy sound. Apart from the opening stomper, 'Hello', with its aural and lyrical references to

Liam greets the paparazzi

Gary Glitter's 'Hello, Hello, I'm Back Again', the rocky 'Hey Now!', the clattering 45-seconds of 'Swamp Song' and the jokey 'She's Electric' (not forgetting, of course, 'Roll With It' and 'Some Might Say'), the mood of '(What's The Story) Morning Glory?' was downbeat; some of the tracks verged on the elegiacal - not bad for a band considered by some to be a bunch of yobboes with hardly an ounce of soul or poetry between them.

dehumanising society – by turns sad and bitter, it was possibly Noel's most directly autobiographical song to date, apparently a meditation on the negative aspects of (his) success. The album's closing song, 'Champagne Supernova', was another sorrowful comment on life in the eye of the Oasis hurricane during the band's astonishing rise to prominence: the track, which immediately assumed classic status among Oasis fans, particularly for its

made/When you're chained to the mirror and the razor blade'). 'Morning Glory' outstripped virtually every rock song of the last 20 years, its breathtaking five minutes rivalling anything by the unholy noisy trinity – The Stooges, The Stones and The Sex Pistols.

The reviews of the album in the music press were lukewarm, but that didn't stop it entering the charts at Number One and becoming the fastest selling LP since Michael Jackson's 'Bad' in 1987, shifting

Of the moody numbers, 'Wonderwall' was a semi-acoustic beauty that also featured cello and some gloriously soulful, rasping vocals from Liam. 'Don't Look Back In Anger' was instantly memorable, a grandiose ballad lovingly sung by Noel with a piano intro lifted directly from John Lennon's 'Imagine' and a set of lyrics that referred to John and Yoko's historic 'bedin' protests from the early Seventies. 'Cast No Shadow' was another beautifully melodic epitaph for a man stripped of his soul and pride by a

memorable, 'Where were you when we were getting high?' refrain, which grew to a mindblowing climax that was pure 'Live Forever' meets 'Hey Jude'.

Best of all, though, was the enormously compelling penultimate track, 'Morning Glory': starting with some 'Apocalypse Now!' helicopter blades and jagged guitars, it soon crashed into a soaring, searing rush of melody and noise that served to underpin the ambiguously pro-hedonist – and tabloidbaiting – lyric ('All your dreams are

around 350,000 copies in its first week in the shops. And with 'Roll With It', 'Some Might Say' plus future singles 'Wonderwall' and 'Don't Look Back In Anger' (as well as four other potential hit singles in 'Morning Glory', 'Cast No Shadow', 'Hello' and 'Champagne Supernova'), '(What's The Story) Morning Glory?' virtually amounted to Oasis' second 'Greatest Hits' compilation in two years.

The writers of those lukewarm reviews had a job cleaning all the egg off their faces by the end of the year.

Message for the Nineties – Oasis writ large

HIGHER THAN THE SCUM

AND then they got really successful. In November, Oasis broke yet another record, playing two nights at London's Earl's Court before 19,000 people per show, the highest ever figure for an indoor concert. The gigs brought the stars out in their droves: Bono, The Edge and Adam Clayton from U2; James Dean Bradfield of The Manic Street Preachers; ex-Take That boy wonder and friend of the Gallaghers, Robbie Williams; snooker supremo Alex Higgins; Simon and Yasmin Le Bon; Paula Yates and Michael Hutchence; The Beautiful South; George Michael; Primal Scream; Mrs Jim 'Simple Minds' Kerr/future girlfriend of Liam Gallagher, Patsy Kensit; Pulp; Kylie Minogue; and Neil Tennent of The Pet Shop Boys. Only The Rolling Stones and The Who, who were allegedly on the band's after-show guest-list, didn't make an appearance. Apart from them, it seemed as though everybody who was anybody on Planet Pop wanted to be seen to

be seen at The Scene That Celebrates Oasis.

By December, the increasingly rich Noel Gallagher was guaranteed yet more songwriting royalties, and achieved another first, when his song, 'Wonderwall', appeared in the singles charts not once, but twice. One version was on the latest EP by his band (featuring the sublime extra track, 'The Masterplan', proving once and for all that Noel throws away songs good enough for

most bands to base careers around); the other was a gently ironic yet affectionate Easy/Cheesy Listening rendition from the post-modern Ray Conniff Orchestra – The Mike Flowers Pops Orchestra. Both versions reached Number Two. Touchingly, a report reached *Melody Maker's* news desk around this time that the haunting 'Wonderwall' had been played at the funeral of Oasis fan, Leah Betts, the teenager who tragically died in late

'95 after taking the drug Ecstasy.

Oasis had plenty to celebrate at Christmas. So did Creation Records, which is probably why record company boss Alan McGee gave Noel Gallagher a Roll's Royce as a show of his gratitude for all the money the songwriter had made on his behalf in what had been easily the long-established record company's most successful year to date. Unfortunately, Noel had yet to pass his driving test, although, of course, 'Pop stars don't drive – they get driven,' as he told a passing journalist.

It wouldn't be long before McGee recouped on his generous gift. The fourth single from '(What's The Story) Morning Glory?' was 'Don't Look Back In Anger', and it came backed with 'Step Out' (which was originally due to appear on the album, and was noticeably co-credited to one Stevie Wonder, so similar was the chorus to Wonder's much-loved 'Uptight'), as well as the rousing 'Underneath The Sky' and one more nod to Noel's glam roots, a version of Slade's bootboy classic, 'Cum On Feel The Noize'. Released in February 1996, 'Don't Look Back In Anger' went straight in at Number One.

This was no surprise considering the amount of publicity Oasis received during the week leading up to the release of the single. At the 1996 Brit Awards ceremony, there were more controversial happenings than at any media event in living memory. Due to the silly-bugger antics of Pulp's Jarvis Cocker (who clambered onstage and acted the goat during Michael 'I Am The Son Of God' Jackson's pseudo-cataclysmic performance of 'Earth Song), and due to some spectacularly surly behaviour from the Gallagher brothers, the ghost of Bill Grundy could at last be laid to rest. Not content with winning three awards (for Best Band, Best Video and Best Album), Noel declared that 'has-beens shouldn't be presenting fucking awards to gonna-be's' after Michael Hutchence handed over a statuette for 'Wonderwall'. Liam then proceeded to bend over, show his rear to the crowd and pretend to stick the statuette where the sun rarely shines. The Brothers Grim then embarked on an alternative version of Blur's 'Parklife', wittily retitled 'Shitelife', before confusingly proclaiming, 'Power to the people!' only moments after taunting the populace for being poor while he, on the other hand, was stinking rich.

Liam and Noel with Michael Hutchence at the Brits '96

Still, Noel could afford to be smug: by the first week of March 1996, Oasis were not only Number One in Britain, they were also Number Three in the States with '(What's The Story) Morning Glory?', disproving at a stroke the long-held theory that Britpop could not be sold to the Americans.

Only two years after boasting to whomsoever cared to listen that Oasis were going to be the biggest band in the world, Noel Gallagher had achieved the unachievable. Now all they had to do was colonise Venus and Mars and they could take over the rest of the galaxy. Stranger things have happened.

Oasis make friends with Ronnie Wood at the *Q Magazine* awards

★★★★★★ ★★★★★★

'Upsetting Sons'

HOT GOSSIP

INCREDIBLY, although Oasis only released one record in 1996 – 'Don't Look Back In Anger' – their presence in the media and in the public's imagination was stronger than ever throughout the year.

The year began with the Australian branch of Oasis' fanclub promising to launch a petition to get their favourite band to perform down under. And the clothing company Gloverall reported a 20 per cent surge in sales of duffel coats thanks to the Gallagher brothers, who wore said fashion items at Glastonbury and on the sleeve of 'Roll With It'.

Meanwhile, Courtney Love, the widow of Nirvana's Kurt Cobain, was posting anti-Oasis messages on the Internet, inciting fans of her band, Hole, to boycott Oasis' records and pleading with them not to buy tickets for Oasis' spring American tour.

The same month, rumours started circulating that Noel Gallagher was to write the debut solo single for Robbie Williams, erstwhile podgy song-and-dance-man with Take That. Reports also claimed that Oasis had vetoed plans for cartoon blue midgets, The Smurfs, to record versions of 'Wonderwall', 'Roll With It' and 'Some Might Say' under the titles 'Wondersmurf', 'Smurf

With It' and 'Some Might Smurf'. More hearsay suggested that 'All Around The World', a supremely catchy song that Noel had namechecked in interviews for a while now, was to be Oasis' entry in 1996's Eurovision Song Contest!

In a more serious development, a story in the *News Of The World* featured reports – exaggerated ones, it later transpired – of events surrounding Oasis' two weekend gigs at Dublin's The Point at the end of March. First, the paper stated that Liam fought on the floor of Dublin's Westbury Hotel with his estranged father, Tommy, after the Saturday show, and that up to 50 police were called. In fact, according to an Oasis spokesman, Tommy Gallagher and a *News Of The World* reporter arrived at the hotel and tried to goad Liam into reacting, but the star refused to lose his cool.

The night before, if the aforementioned tabloid was to be believed, Liam's turbulent relationship with Patsy Kensit was almost irreparably damaged. Allegedly, Liam had been flirting with former *Brookside* actress Anna Friel, which led to a furious argument with Patsy, after which she reputedly threw his clothes out of the hotel window, and he trashed the room. The row couldn't have been too fierce, however, because, exactly twelve months later, Liam and Patsy would be married.

Arguably Oasis' biggest impact to date on the British media came in late March, and it was all due to a seemingly harmless interview with a journalist from *Melody Maker*. As Features Editor with the paper at the time I decided to send writer Ben Stud and photographer Tom Sheehan to America, where Oasis were touring.

As soon as Noel and Liam clapped eyes on Sheehan and Stud hanging outside the Philadelphia Tower, where Oasis were due to play that night, the Gallaghers invited the *'Maker* backstage for an informal chat.

It was during this encounter with Oasis' most ardent champions in the UK music press that Noel felt sufficiently relaxed to open up about his past, and his occasional bouts of bad, even illegal, behaviour.

'What people have to understand is that we are lads,' said Noel, wearing a badge that had been given to him by a fan, which proudly proclaimed: 'The Greatest Rock'N'Roll Band In The World'. 'We have burgled houses and nicked car stereos, and we like girls and we swear and go to the football and take the piss. Sometimes we get carried away.'

It was the line about 'burgling houses', delivered in typically nonchalant Noel Gallagher style, that did it. No sooner had that issue of *Melody Maker* hit the news-

Patsy and Liam make a break for it

stands than anti-porn campaigner, Dr Adrian Rogers of the Conservative Family Institute, was calling for a total ban on all Oasis product, claiming the band exerted a pernicious, evil influence on the innocent youth of Great Britain.

Ben Stud and myself spent the next two weeks speaking to reporters from radio, TV and the press, defending Noel's comments – and his profligate use of the 'f' word – in everything from *The Times* to *The Daily Mirror*, on everything from BBC Radio Scotland to Greater Manchester Radio.

My appearance on the latter was especially significant since the Manchester

police were now threatening to open an investigation into Noel Gallagher's 10-year-old delinquent activities. Ben Stud even found himself having to account for the tapes of his interview with Gallagher, in a series of informal conversations with CID Chief Superintendent David James.

Absurd but true.

THE MAINE ATTRACTION

RATHER less controversial, although just as newsworthy, were the emotional Oasis concerts at Manchester City's Maine Road football ground on April 27 and 28, when a total of 80,000 people witnessed the band triumph in the home stadium of their beloved soccer team.

On Saturday April 27, 40,000 devotees flocked from all over the country, Europe, the world, to watch Oasis play at home and to turn drab, dreary Moss Side into the most magical place on earth. Forty thousand lost souls came together to sing, 'All your dreams are made/When you're chained to the mirror and the razor blade, and to form some kind of joyous union likened by *MM*'s Everett True to a bonding of religiously ecstatic proportions. 'An acceptable kind of holiness,' he called it.

By all accounts, Oasis' Maine Road performance the following night was even better, the band stepping up several gears and avoiding any of the sloppiness and inconsistency which occasionally spoil their shows. Liam even bowed down to a giant black and white image of John Lennon that flashed up on a screen at the back of the stage, so confident that he could afford to pay homage to the one man whose supreme talent, in Liam's supremely arrogant opinion, would have given him cause to worry, had he not been gunned down in 1980.

'Oasis embody everything great about rock'n'roll – celebration, hedonism, unashamed masculinity, top tunes, the lot,' said Everett True.

As for Noel Gallagher, he was equally succinct as he left the stage that night: 'Goodbye from the best band in the world to the best fans in the world.'

SUMMER MADNESS

OASIS were to eclipse their own enormous achievements with regard to live extravaganzas by August 1996.

First, though, the band kept themselves busy, and their profile high in the papers, with a series of public activities and confrontational gestures.

In May, Noel and his nemesis, Damon Albarn of Blur, stayed away from the Ivor Novello Awards ceremony after they had both been declared Songwriter Of The Year.

Noel continued to get up the authorities' noses in June when, after 'Don't Look Back In Anger' had been accepted by German TV bosses as the official anthem for all their Euro '96 coverage but rejected by their UK counterparts in favour of 'Ode To Joy' by Beethoven, a spokesman from Creation said: 'Oasis are delighted that the Germans, at least, are saying, "Roll Over Beethoven." '

By mid-June, it was official: Oasis were bigger than The Beatles. According to a survey conducted by the music industry magazine *Music Week*, 15 to 45 year olds in seven major British cities decided that Oasis were the country's favourite act, by an 'overwhelming' majority.

In July, Noel entered the spotlight of another all-time great when he joined legendary easy-listening tunesmith Burt Bacharach (who, of course, had featured on the front cover of 'Definitely Maybe') on stage at London's Royal Festival Hall for a rendition of 'This Guy's In Love With You', the song about which Noel once said, had he written it, he would die happy. And more importantly, Noel's appearance confirmed Oasis' cross-generational appeal.

'It seriously was stunning,' said a record company spokesman. 'Liam and Patsy were up on their feet, cheering.'

Noel got involved in another collaboration in July, right at the other end of the musical spectrum: with warped-beat psychedelic techno duo, The Chemical Brothers. 'Setting Sun', the Gallagher-Chemicals team-up which took its cue from The Beatles' 'Tomorrow Never Knows' (arguably the first ever psychedelic pop song) and added huge,

pumping dance rhythms, featured a crazed, druggy-sounding vocal from Noel. Not surprisingly, despite its uncompromising nature, 'Setting Sun' entered the charts at Number One. It wasn't Noel's only dance-related collaboration of the year, either: within three months, Beck's 'Devil's Haircut' enhanced by a Noel remix, became the American star's biggest hit to date

In August, 'What's The Story (Morning Glory)' was shortlisted for 1996's Mercury Prize, along with Pulp's 'Different Class', Manic Street Preachers' 'Everything Must Go', Black Grape's 'It's Great When You're Straight. . . Yeah!', Underworld's 'Second Toughest In The Infants' and Mark Morrison's 'Return Of The Mack' and the all-star 'Help' charity album.

The latter LP eventually won, desrvedly so considering the cause, although any disappoint Oasis may have felt will have been tempered by their album's sales, which, to date, place it behind only 'Sgt Pepper' and Michael Jackson's 'Bad' in the British all-time best-sellers lists – three million copies and rising.

LOCH'N'ROLL!

IN eight days in August 1996, Oasis played in front of 350,000 people. On one weekend, they appeared in front of 80,000 euphoric revellers. This turned out to be the biggest warm-up in the history of popular music. Because, the following weekend, the band performed in a field in Hertfordshire, and more than a quarter of a million people turned up for what remains the biggest single rock'n'roll event of the Nineties, Britain's very own Woodstock. The difference between the hippy festival of the Sixties and Oasis at Knebworth is simple: this time the enormous audience had travelled in their droves from far and wide for just one band.

The shows at Loch Lomond in Scotland actually had more in common with Altamont, the 1969 rock festival which ended the hippy dream after a man got stabbed during The Rolling Stones' performance of 'Sympathy For The Devil'. Because, before Oasis even

Liam at Knebworth

started tuning up, three people had died in various motor accidents, including, most tragically for the band because he was a personal friend, Rob Collins the keyboard player with The Charlatans

Somehow, Oasis managed to wring beauty from these tragedies. For starters, there were the engagement rings being worn – and shown off – by Patsy (a square diamond in a plain gold band) and Liam (an Irish Claddah-style friendship ring of two clasped hands with a ruby as the centrepiece). As for the gigs, they were predictably marvellous. Ably supported by Cast, Manic Street Preachers and Black Grape, Oasis never once looked as though they were anything but in control, refusing to be swayed by the sheer size of the venture, simply as magnificent as the crowd was enormous.

They even played two brand new songs – 'My Big Mouth' and 'It's Getting Better Man' – which proved that Noel Gallagher's grasp of this songwriting lark was as sure as ever. 'You've read about The Who, the Stones, the Pistols . . .' wrote Dave Simpson in the *Melody Maker* '. . . they're past tense. Oasis are here for you now. Make the most of them.'

WE ARE NOT KNEBWORTHY!

KNEBWORTH, of course, made Loch Lomond and pretty much every other major rock concert in recent history seem like a dress rehearsal.

Over two days, a quarter of a million people stood in a damp field twenty or so miles north of London to watch five men who, just over two years before, were attracting the proverbial two blokes and a mutt to their gigs.

The statistics surrounding Knebworth are as mindblowing as Oasis' music. The two shows together generated more than £5 million. More than two million people – nearly four per cent of the population – applied for tickets. Tickets sold out within eight hours of the first telephone line opening. The cost of policing the event was £400,000. Over 50 miles of cable were required to supply roughly the amount of electricity used in a day by a town the size of Milton Keynes. The 100 square metre Digiwall video screen was the largest ever built. The audience for either show, layed head to toe, would have stretched from Burnage to Knebworth. The shows were broadcast live on radio to 34 countries and 300 million people.

The gig itself just about lived up the hyperbole and statistics (even if it did take some people several hours to leave the site and get home, so jammed-packed was it with the 38,000 or so cars and 1,500 coaches). The sense of excitement provided by the band (helped by ex-Stone Roses guitarist John Squire on 'Champagne Supernova' and the perennial rendition of The Beatles' 'I Am The Walrus') – not forgetting the breathtaking firework display at the climax – was, if anything, heightened by the sheer scale of it all, the feeling of being part of an audience who were not just watching but taking part in history as it was being made.

As for Oasis, they shrugged off their staggering achievement: 'This isn't the culmination of anything,' said their manager, Marcus Russell. 'Nor is it the beginning of anything. We are merely satisfying the huge demand for concert tickets to see Oasis.'

OASIS UNPLUGGED

THE demand to see Oasis film an MTV *Unplugged* at a secret location (it turned out to be The Royal Festival Hall) at the end of August may have been huge, but only 400 lucky punters were fortunate enough to be present. The set itself followed the usual *Unplugged* acoustic-based guidelines, but the problem was, Liam Gallagher was highly conspicuous by his absence.

Not that Liam wasn't down at The Royal Festival Hall that night – he was. It's just that he wasn't where he was meant to be, on stage. Instead, he was in one of those 'boxes' above the stage reserved for royalty or superstars, canoodling with Patsy and generally refusing to sing with the band. Immediate worries that Liam and Noel had had one of their spats were alleviated by a sardonic message from the elder Gallagher as he took to the stage.

'Liam's got a sore throat, so you're going to have to make do with the four ugly ones,' he said, to the palpable disappointment of the 400-strong crowd, who had come to be bowled over by Liam's charisma as much as by his brother's songs. MTV themselves weren't exactly delighted, either.

Oasis nearly became completely unplugged in September. The band threatened to take legal action against certain papers who alleged that Liam Gallagher had been seeing a therapist. Then there was the story that hogged the headlines in the very same week that seven Iraqi asylum-seekers hijacked a plane at Stansted airport: Liam missed one of the band's shows on their latest tour of the States. Even that bastion of all things weighty and serious, *Newsnight*, saw Jeremy Paxman forced to address this relatively piffling little matter.

Liam's sudden decision not to board the plane for Oasis' ninth tour of America was blamed on the fact that he was house-hunting with Patsy. 'You're all wankers,' he told the gaggles of hacks as he strolled through Heathrow Airport, flanked by two minders. 'I fucking hate you lot.'

He had another run in later the same month when, at the MTV Video Music Awards, broadcast live to 300 million people worldwide, he knocked over his microphone, sang 'Up yer bum!' during 'Champagne Supernova', spat, tossed a can of beer into the air, and then walked off.

Oasis, Knebworth '96 – the encore

JUST SAY NOEL

OASIS' final brush with the authorities came at the end of 1996, spilled over into 1997, and was arguably the most serious of all. In November Liam was not only involved in a fight with a journalist over a photograph of him 'canoodling with another woman' (*News Of The World*), he was also alleged to have bitten the nose of a young woman. Last but by no means least of these unfortunate incidents occured when Liam was arrested in London's Oxford Street on suspicion of possessing drugs.

On a happier note, Oasis won The Best Band In The World Today trophy at the *Q* Awards, and 'Wonderwall' was voted best song of all time by Radio 1's listeners, just ahead of Nirvana's 'Smells Like Teen Spirit' and The Prodigy's 'Firestarter'.

In fact, 1997 was far less fraught than '96, the year in which, according to David Bennun of *Loaded* magazine, 'Oasis became the one thing the country had in common.' For several weeks, the press were reduced to featuring shock-horror front page articles on – gasp! – Liam and Noel's new haircuts. And then, on April 7th, Liam and Patsy finally tied the knot after a few false starts designed to put the hellhounds of the media off the scent, and Paul McGuigan married his girlfriend in St Lucia.

Music-wise (remember that?), Oasis spent March recording a series of cover versions as bonus tracks for the singles that were to be lifted from their third album, whose working title was 'Be Here Now'.

Among them was a version of The Beatles' 'Helter Skelter', notorious in the Sixties for reputedly 'inspiring' hippy murderer Charles Manson to kill actress Sharon Tate. The band also recorded a version of David Bowie's 1977 hit, 'Heroes'.

In May, *Melody Maker* reported that Oasis' new single, their first since February '96 and due for release on July 7th (three weeks after the band's dates at San Francisco's Oakland Stadium with U2, on the latter's 'Pop Mart' tour of the globe), was to be called 'D'You Know What I Mean?' The seven-inch and cassette formats would feature 'D'You Know What I Mean?' and an extra new track 'Stay Young', both with lead vocals by Liam, while the 12-inch was to contain 'Angel Child', sung by Noel, and the digipak CD would include 'Heroes'.

A source close to the band described the single as being 'not a ballad, but it's not "Roll With It" either,' adding 'Oasis fans will totally love it.'

As will, presumably, most of the rest of the planet.

August '96, Liam at Chicago airport

Liam sits this one out during the American tour